The *2-hour* TAROT TUTOR

The *2-hour* TAROT TUTOR

*The fast, revolutionary
method for learning to read
tarot cards in 2 hours*

WILMA CARROLL

PIATKUS

Visit the Piatkus website!

Piatkus publishes a wide range of best-selling fiction and non-fiction, including books on health, mind, body & spirit, sex, self-help, cookery, biography and the paranormal.

If you want to:

- read descriptions of our popular titles
- buy our books over the Internet
- take advantage of our special offers
- enter our monthly competition
- learn more about your favourite Piatkus authors

VISIT OUR WEBSITE AT: www.piatkus.co.uk

First published in Great Britain in 2005 by
Piatkus Books Ltd
5 Windmill Street, London W1T 2JA
email: info@piatkus.co.uk

The moral right of the author has been asserted

A catalogue record for this book is available from the British Library

ISBN 0 7499 2610 4

Text design by Tiffany Estreicher
Illustrations from the Rider-Waite Tarot Deck, known also as the Rider Tarot and the Waite Tarot, reproduced by permission of U.S. Games Systems, Inc., Stamford, Connecticut, 06902 USA. Copyright 1971 by U.S. Games Systems, Inc. Further reproduction prohibited. The Rider-Waite Tarot Deck is a registered trademark of U.S. Games Systems, Inc.

This book has been printed on paper manufactured
with respect for the environment using wood from
managed sustainable resources

Typeset in Great Britain by Phoenix Photosetting, Chatham, Kent
Printed and bound in Great Britain by Mackays of Chatham Ltd

To My Beloved Aunt Dorothy

CONTENTS

NOTICE

This method is guaranteed to work if the instructions are followed in the exact order in which they are presented! Do NOT refer to the other chapters until the exercises in THE FIRST 2 HOURS have been correctly completed!

ACKNOWLEDGMENTS

My deepest gratitude firstly goes to my agent, Mary Tahan, and my editor, Christine Zika. They were the two very powerful forces behind this book.

Special thanks to graphic designer Michele Monteforte; Peter Gray Cohen for biographical information on the late Eden Gray; Lynn M. Buess for allowing me to include his wonderful Tarot spreads (Five-By-Five and Yes or No); the late Richard Gardner for his Tarot spread (Past, Present, and Future) and Magenta Wise for giving me permission to include it.

Much appreciation for the help I received from the guys at Copy Cats: Rob, Jim, and Komo; and many thanks to George Keskeny and Tammy Mauriello for those little extras.

I shall be eternally indebted to the many spiritual teachers I met along the way, who answered my unending questions, indulged me in my youthful exuberance, and always encouraged me in my spiritual pursuits.

I am also grateful to the many people whose feedback over

the years helped me to navigate the course of my Tarot card readings and the development of my teachings.

I believe everyone can read Tarot cards. It is really an open secret, and now I share it with the world. This gift was made possible because of all the others who generously shared their knowledge and inspiration with me.

INTRODUCTION:
STOP, LOOK, LISTEN!

It was 2 A.M. I had been shuffling and throwing the cards since 10 P.M. With each spread, I would look up the meanings in books. I had been repeating this same ritual for weeks. I was trying in vain to learn how to read Tarot cards.

A sophomore in college, I had an English Lit class at 8:30 A.M. I was exhausted and had to get some sleep, but I couldn't stop. Forcing myself, I gathered the cards together and placed them in a glittering antique beaded bag. It was intended *solely* for them. I set it high on a shelf.

As I lay in bed, hovering between consciousness and sleep, the cards began to rise up in my thoughts and the images danced in my mind. Last week the 3 of Cups had come up two times, falling in the position of the *home*. Then I remembered several friends had made a surprise visit to my apartment. Five days ago, The Lovers came up in the position of the *future*. The following day a guy I had been interested in asked me out.

More and more pictures swirled through my head, appearing

before me as reminders, describing something that had recently happened in my life. What I began to realize was that the cards were actually talking to me. In fact, they had always been talking to me *through the pictures*, only I had not been listening. Finally, sleep overtook me.

The next day, my classes were over by 12:30 P.M. I rushed back home with no intention of studying. Pulling the cards from the shelf, I grabbed all the Tarot books and put *them* on the shelf. I was going to read the cards *without* the books. I was going to look *only* at the cards. What was in the pictures? What did I see? Eureka! That was the whole key! Look at the *cards*, not in the *books*!

The *2-hour* TAROT TUTOR

ONE PICTURE IS WORTH A THOUSAND WORDS

PART A: E-Z THREE CARD SPREAD
Every Picture Tells a Story

James sat before me spellbound. He was a business major at a competitive university on Long Island, New York.

"How do you do it?" he wondered aloud.

"It's easy!" I assured him.

I pulled a card from the deck, the Knight of Cups.

"Look at the card. What do you see?" I asked. "Say what you see in the card," I instructed.

At first he was bashful about it, but I insisted.

"Make something up!" I urged.

James quickly gave a description.

"I see a man riding a horse. He's carrying a cup. There are wings on his helmet and on his heels." (See Figure 1.1.)

KNIGHT of CUPS.

FIGURE 1.1
Knight of Cups
Look at the card. Say what you see in the card: A man is riding a horse. He carries a cup. There are wings on his helmet and on his heels.

I then pulled another card, the 3 of Cups. I asked him to repeat the same exercise.

"Look at the card. Say what you see in the card," I instructed again.

James gave another description of this card.

"I see three women dancing and holding cups. They're partying!" he said, laughing. (See Figure 1.2.)

FIGURE 1.2
3 of Cups
Look at the card. Say what you see in the card: Three women dancing and holding cups. It's a party.

I then pulled a third card, the 2 of Cups, and repeated the same instructions.

"It looks like a married couple," he answered. (See Figure 1.3.)

FIGURE 1.3

2 of Cups
Look at the card. Say what you see in the card: Two people in love or a married couple.

After that, I laid the three cards side-by-side. I instructed James to make up a story about the three cards all together.

"Someone carries a message about a wedding party. An invitation to a wedding!" he blurted.

I informed James he had just given his first Tarot card reading and all he had to do was *look at the cards*!

KNIGHT of CUPS.

Let's try the same exercise using a set of three different cards. **Look at the cards and say what you see.** Make *free associations* with the images. Be spontaneous and go with the first thing that comes to mind!

Look at the card. Say what you see in the card: A man is working. (See Figure 1.4.)

FIGURE 1.4
8 of Pentacles

Look at the card. Say what you see in the card. What comes to your mind immediately: A man is fighting against something. (See Figure 1.5.)

FIGURE 1.5
7 of Wands

Look at the card. Say what you see in the card: A terrible fight or a violent argument. (See Figure 1.6.)

FIGURE 1.6
5 of Swords

Now, look at the three cards side-by-side. Weave what you have seen in each card into a story. Incorporate the *key words* you used to describe them: work, fights, bad arguments. How about something like this: Arguments and power struggles where one works.

Here's another example. This time try it *without* any hints. Remember to **look at the card. Say what you see in the card.** Go with what immediately comes into your mind. *Free associate.* Then move on to the next card.

QUEEN of PENTACLES.

Look at the card. Say what you see in the card.

THE LOVERS.

Look at the card. Say what you see in the card.

Now weave what you see in these cards into a story or inter-pretation. Make *free associations* with the images. Use *key words* to describe them.

Perhaps you see an introspective woman who is thinking of walking away from a troubling romance. Or maybe you see a woman who is disappointed about a relationship or thinking about giving up on love completely. You may even see a woman reading a sad book about an unfulfilling or unrequited romance. All of these interpretations can be correct. Or you may see something totally different from what I am suggesting. Certainly other interpretations are also possible. But, it is important to go with the *first* impression that pops into your mind. A good cop will agree: *Your first hunch is usually your best.*

Dion Fortune was one of the most famous and prolific occult writers of the twentieth century. In her book, *Practical Occultism in Daily Life*, she wrote how, with any form of divination, the interpretation [must] "leap spontaneously to the mind . . ." Always go with what instantaneously comes to your mind. This is a very important key to reading Tarot cards.

Reading Tarot cards is really very easy. All you have to do is **look at the cards and say what you see**! By simply looking at the cards, you are making an intuitive connection with them. The cards speak in a language of symbols. If you look at the cards, the images actually do talk to you.

This is a truly revolutionary technique. I break all the rules. And here is a trade secret: so do *all* the really *good* readers. They are not following the standard rules either.

With my radical method, there is no memorizing of meanings, no years and years of studying; nor do you even have to think. Instead, you will be able to develop your own meanings to the cards spontaneously if you immediately get into the habit of looking at the cards and saying what you see. These instructions will be repeated throughout the book. Constant repetition is what helps the mind get past the resistance of preconceived ideas. If you have already been trying to figure out the Tarot, you most likely have several preconceived ideas about the cards and may have built up a resistance to this new approach. Clear your mind. Start afresh. And always remember to **look at the cards and say what you see**!

The exercises in the following section are more in-depth. **Follow the instructions exactly the way they are presented!**

NOTICE

**Follow These Instructions
In the *Exact* Order
In Which They Are Presented!**

Do *Not* Skip Ahead!

**Do *Not* Refer to the Other Chapters
Until the Exercises in**

The First 2 Hours

Have Been Correctly Completed!

**This Method is *Guaranteed* to Work
If the Instructions
Are Followed *Sequentially*.**

PART B: THE FIRST 2 HOURS
Getting There Is Half the Fun!

✳ **SECTION 1: THE INITIAL EXERCISE**

Marie showed me all of her Tarot books.

"They're so confusing," she complained. "I can't figure them out!"

Having just entered her freshman year at a college in Pennsylvania, she was well-acquainted with Tarot cards. Her mother had consulted many readers while Marie was growing up in New Jersey. By her mother's side for many of these sessions, Marie watched with burning curiosity, wondering how it was done.

Now she was determined to *crack the code* herself and maybe even save her mother some money. But Marie had fallen into the trap of looking up the meanings in books, trying to memorize them; and, she found all of the instructions too complicated to understand.

"These books give me a headache!" she complained.

"Put the books away," I instructed. I gathered them together and set them off to the side.

And these are the same instructions I now give to all of you Tarot enthusiasts. Put your Tarot books away; all of them. Put them high on a shelf, out of reach. You will not be needing them. All you need now is your deck of Rider-Waite Tarot Cards.

You are going to start with the first card. If you have just taken the deck out of the package, the cards will be in order and the first will be The Magician. If you have been playing with them for awhile (and I expect you have) it is *not* necessary to put them in order. You can start with whichever card is on top.

PICK UP A CARD AND LOOK AT IT. SAY WHAT YOU SEE IN THE CARD. Quickly say *one* thing you see in the card. Be spontaneous, do *not think* about it; instead, say whatever immediately comes to mind. You may see a man standing with outstretched arms. *Say what you see.* You may see someone sitting under a tree staring at cups. *Say what you see.*

Say at least one thing you see or as many as three things; but, be very quick. Do not pause or hesitate. Do *not* stop to think. Spontaneously and quickly, SAY WHAT YOU SEE IN THE CARD. Then move onto to the next card, repeating the same exercise until you have gone through all seventy-eight Tarot cards *very quickly.* Be *spontaneous* and *speedy.*

NOW PUT THE BOOK DOWN.
LOOK ONLY AT THE CARDS WHILE
DOING THIS EXERCISE.
DO NOT PICK UP THE BOOK UNTIL YOU HAVE
COMPLETED THIS EXERCISE.

IF YOU HAVE COMPLETED THE
EXERCISE ABOVE, YOU MAY CONTINUE WITH THE
FOLLOWING EXERCISE.

Now you are going to repeat the same exercise; except this time at a slower pace. Look closer and longer at the cards. Take some time to notice more details in the pictures. Look for something you did not see before. Here are some examples to get you started.

TEMPERANCE: An angel stands with one foot in the water and one foot on the ground. Water is poured from chalice to chalice. To his right, a path leads to the sun in the background.

THE STAR: A woman has one foot in the water and a knee on the ground. She pours water into the water and onto the ground. Behind her is a bird perched in a tree.

THE FOOL: A man looks to the sky while stepping off a cliff. A dog barks at his foot. He holds a flower in his left hand.

QUEEN OF PENTACLES: A rabbit scoots by to the left of her throne. (You have to look closely for this. Even the Queen *herself* does not see it.)

10 OF PENTACLES: In the foreground sits an older man looking on. (This is another one you have to look for closely.)

KING OF WANDS: A man sits on a throne. Leaves sprout out of the wand he is holding. A tiny lizard sits to his left.

7 OF WANDS: A man wears a shoe on his right foot and a boot on his left foot.

QUEEN OF SWORDS: A woman sits on a throne. Her left hand is slightly raised. She stares off into the distance. Only her profile is visible, *not* her entire face.

PAGE OF SWORDS: A young man appears to be leaning to his left, but looks to his right. The top of the sword he holds is missing. Birds fly above.

9 OF SWORDS: Astrological symbols and roses cover the blanket. On the panel, below the bed, appear to be two men fighting. (Here is another one you must look at *very* closely.)

6 OF SWORDS: To the left of the boat, the water is calm; to the right, the water is rippled.

Your responses should still be quick and spontaneous. Take only a few minutes with each card. Go through all seventy-eight cards again. **Look at the cards and say what you see.**

**NOW PUT THE BOOK DOWN AGAIN.
DO NOT PICK IT UP UNTIL
YOU HAVE COMPLETED THIS EXERCISE.**

I hope you have completed the above-exercises exactly as I have instructed. These exercises are very important. They lay the foundation for all your future work with Tarot cards. By *looking* at the cards you are allowing your subconscious mind to make an intuitive link with the Tarot's symbolism, and you are already beginning *naturally* to develop your own meanings to the cards. In other words, when you *look* at the picture, you intuitively *get the picture*. This is an ongoing process. As you continuously look at a Tarot card over the years, you will likely see something different and revise its meaning.

Spontaneity is the essential key. It unlocks your *intuitive/ psychic faculties* by facilitating the shift from logical thinking to intuitive perception. Rational thinking interferes with the intuitive mind. If you depend on your rational (thinking) mind to read the cards, it will be an exercise in futility. Spontaneity, *not* thinking, engages the intuition, which lets impressions flow smoothly. This brings insights instantly to conscious awareness and works in harmony with the true essence of Tarot cards.

PART B: THE FIRST 2 HOURS
Getting There Is Half the Fun!

✴ SECTION 2: THE READING

Sean fidgeted with the cards. He was about to give himself his first Tarot reading.

"I'm a little nervous about this," he confided.

"No need to be," I assured him.

This is the same assurance I give to all of you Tarot aficionados. You will still continue with the basic exercise: *Look at the cards and say what you see*, except this time the cards will have particular placements.

It has been my observation that this is where many people begin to experience extreme confusion. I am going to eliminate that by giving you another trade secret. Skilled readers are not thinking about the cards' positions in a spread. Skilled readers are *looking at (reading) the cards*. This is exactly what I have been teaching you. Keep this secret in the back of your mind when following the next set of instructions. The various spreads used for Tarot card reading are designed to give the reader some direction. It is the cards themselves that will ultimately do the talking!

There are countless spreads that can be used, but the most popular is the Celtic Cross Spread.

1. The first step is to select what is called a *significator.* This is the card used to represent the person getting the reading. That individual is called the *querent.* The significator is usually a court card that best describes the appearance of the querent. Here are some *suggested guidelines* for this selection:

Black hair or very dark hair, dark eyes—Pentacles
Blond or very light hair, blue or light eyes—Cups
Red hair or light brown hair, hazel or brown eyes—Wands
Light, medium, or dark brown hair, gray or light eyes—Swords
A man 35 years of age or older—a king
A woman 35 years of age or older—a queen
A young man 18 to 34 years of age—a knight
A young woman 18 to 34 years of age—a page
A teenager or child (male or female)—a page

I repeat, these are *suggested guidelines* only. You can also select a significator according to *your* own personal taste and style by using whichever card you feel best represents the querent. For a mother you might use The Empress; for a father, The Emperor; a clergyman or very religious individual, The Hierophant; a judge or a lawyer, Justice. Or regardless of appearance, you may see a businesswoman as the Queen of Pentacles or the Queen of Wands; a student as the Page or Knight of Pentacles and so on. Many years ago, a dear friend of mine used to insist *my* significator was The High Priestess.

A significator is *not* necessary. I have been reading Tarot cards for over three decades and stopped using a significator years ago because I felt it did not add to the reading. I know many other professionals who also agree with me. The choice is yours. Tarot card reading is an art; you are the artist.

After you choose a significator, if you choose to do so, put it to the side for the time being. You will be using it when you lay out the cards.

2. The next step is to shuffle the cards. If you have selected a significator, the cards are shuffled *without* it. Remember, keep it aside for now. If you have *not* selected a significator, shuffle the *entire* deck. The querent usually shuffles the cards. However, this is a *practice reading*, so you are going to be the querent and give yourself a reading and shuffle the cards for yourself.

I always say to shuffle the cards until they *feel right*. By this I mean, when one *feels* comfortable with the energy of the cards and that a rapport has been made with them.

There is a theory among bridge players and card sharks that a deck of fifty-two cards must be shuffled seven times to be thoroughly mixed. The Tarot contains seventy-eight cards and could probably use about ten or eleven shuffles.

Unfortunately most people do not shuffle very well; so I suggest you, or the querent, put some energy (or *umpf*) into this procedure and give the cards a really good mixing. You might try relaxing by taking a few deep breaths; then clear your mind as you shuffle. A clear mind makes for a clear reading, even if asking a specific question, which, of course, the Tarot can be used for. However, there will be instructions for that later. For the time being, let's see what comes out. I find this to be one of the most fascinating aspects of the Tarot. Many things are revealed. Future and unexpected events can be seen in the cards, especially when you give them the chance to talk freely. It is easier to hear their voice if the mind is clear when shuffling.

3. After you have thoroughly shuffled the cards, place the deck facedown and with your left hand, going left, cut the deck into three separate piles (See Diagram 1.1). Remember, if you were reading for someone else, the querent would cut the deck. However, *the reader* always picks up the cards after they have been cut by placing one pile on top of the other. With your right hand, pick up pile 1 first. Place it on top of pile number 2 and then place that on top of pile 3. You should now be holding a full deck of Tarot cards in your right hand.

According to tradition, after the querent has cut the deck it should not be touched again by the querent, but handled only by the reader until another spread is done. This is one tradition I am strict about—*my* personal taste. Later on, you can decide for yourself how *you* feel about this tradition.

4. Following Diagram 1.2, lay the cards out faceup. If a significator is used, it is placed down first (faceup), under the card in Position 1. Some readers will say the following words out loud when placing each card in its proper position. It is *not* necessary to say this. Here again, it depends on your personal style. I used to repeat these words many years ago, now I don't. (I want to reemphasize technicalities are not what's really important. They are merely ritualistic and add no magic to the reading. The magic is in the connection you make with the cards by *looking at the cards and saying what you see.*)

Position 1. **"This is what covers you."**
Position 2. **"This is what crosses you."**
Position 3. **"This is above you."**
Position 4. **"This is below you."**
Position 5. **"This is behind you."**

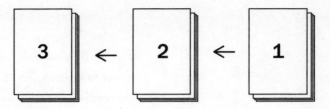

DIAGRAM 1.1

Cut the deck into three separate piles with your left hand, going left. When reading for another person, the querent cuts the deck with the left hand, going left.

Position 6. "This is before you."

Position 7. "This is you."

Position 8. "This is your home, family, friends, and/or environment."

Position 9. "These are your hopes and/or fears."

Position 10. "This is the outcome or culmination."

5. After you have laid the cards out, *quickly* read over the explanation for each position. Do *not* try to memorize this. Do *not* begin referring to the cards in the spread until I give the instructions to do so, and don't worry if you forget everything as soon as you have read it. (I will give more details about this in the next chapter.) Many people tell me they have difficulty remembering these positions; and this is where I see the difficulty beginning. What is most important is to always remember the basic exercise: *Look at the cards and say what you see!* This connects you directly with the cards. After *playing* with the cards for a while, the positions will naturally fall into place. But they will never be as important as the images in the cards themselves.

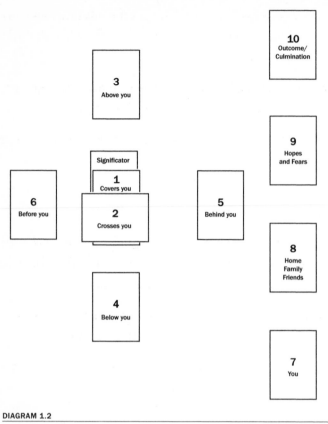

DIAGRAM 1.2

The Celtic Cross Spread

Meanings to the Positions of the Celtic Cross Spread

1. *This Is What Covers You.* This represents the atmosphere or (emotional) environment in which influences are working.

2. *This Is What Crosses You.* This represents an obstacle or an aid.

3. *This Is Above You.* This indicates what the querent is or should be aiming for in the matter. It is sometimes the solution to the issue or the answer to the problem.

4. *This Is Below You.* This describes the subconscious motivation of the querent, how the querent is thinking, or the basis or foundation of the matter.

5. *This Is Behind You.* This represents influences that are now passing away or the immediate or distant past.

6. *This Is Before You.* This is the future or influences that may have recently come into view.

7. *This Is You.* This represents the querent and/or the querent's attitude in the situation.

8. *This Is Your Home, Family, Friends, and/or Environment.* This represents the querent's home, family, friends, or (material) environment or the influences therein.

9. *These Are Your Hopes and/or Fears.* This represents the querent's hopes and/or fears regarding the matter.

10. *This Is the Outcome or Culmination.* This is the way the situation will turn out in the end.

You are now ready to look at the cards in the spread before you. You are going to give yourself a Tarot card reading. **Do not worry about any other details at this time,** even inverted/upside-down cards. I will address that issue and many other questions later on in Chapter 3. At this time, all you have to do is *look at the cards and say what you see.*

Start with the card in Position 1. *Look at the card and say what you see in the card.* Project what you see in the card into the meaning of that position. If you have to refer to the description of this position, do so very quickly, but do *not* get caught up in *thinking* about it. If you have difficulty relating the card to the position, *disregard the position's meaning and focus only on the card and what you see in the card.* Spontaneity is still the order of the day! Quickly move on to Position 2 and repeat the same procedure. Go through all ten positions.

✳   ✳   ✳

Congratulations! You have just given yourself a Tarot card reading. For many of you this was the first time. I know everyone got something out of it. If you have followed these instructions correctly, the entire process should have taken about two hours. However there is much more to be gained! Still focused on the same spread, here are some additional pointers:

■ Be sure to take *dated* notes of the cards that came up in this first reading and *all* your practice spreads. You will most likely be up till the wee hours of the morning like I was, throwing and throwing the cards over and over again. Indeed, a lot can be learned from these initial practice readings. Patterns emerge from the very beginning; the cards really do start talking. By observing these patterns, you can learn the language of the cards. However it is impossible to remember all the cards that come up. That is why the notes make for easy reference. Use the Celtic Cross Spread Worksheet provided at the end of this chapter to record the cards' positions. An extra worksheet for the Celtic Cross Spread is also provided at the end of the book. Make copies and keep them in a Tarot file.

■ Under the worksheet section for *Notes and/or Observations,* keep track of any happenings, occurrences, or events that remind you of the cards that came up in the spread. See what transpires in a few days. Are the events reflected in any of the cards? You will see some very interesting correspondences. These observations will be helpful in further developing your own meanings, because the cards will be talking to you.

Also, in this section, write down any *feelings* you may have had about the cards in the spread. Remember you are beginning to work on an intuitive level and will get *feelings* that contradict rational thinking. Go with your *feelings*!

■ This is only a *practice* reading. Do not take it too seriously and do not lose sleep over it. Eventually, if not right away, you will begin experimenting on your friends and family. Heaven help them! Always be gentle!

There is an old vaudeville joke. Someone asks a taxi driver, "How do you get to Carnegie Hall?"

The driver's answer is "Practice, practice, practice!"

The same is true for learning how to read Tarot cards. *Practice makes perfect*! Continue working with this basic spread. You can use the Celtic Cross Spread for a general reading, to see what comes out. Or you can use it to answer a specific question.

If you wish to advance, there are instructions for a variety of different spreads in further chapters, including worksheets for the most sophisticated, also, in the back of the book. Some spreads may yield enormous amounts of detailed information; others can be used to answer a specific question; or, if you are in a big hurry, there are spreads that give quick and speedy results. Then again, it may boil down to personal taste and style and what you feel comfortable with. Many people work exclusively with the Celtic Cross Spread and have excellent results. The choice is yours.

PERMISSION IS NOW GRANTED TO REFER TO THE OTHER CHAPTERS IN THIS BOOK. You now have a solid foundation for Tarot card reading and are on your way to becoming a highly skilled reader. But, always remember: *Look at the cards and say what you see!* Enjoy!

Celtic Cross Spread Worksheet

Date:_____

Significator _____

1. _____
What Covers You

2. _____
What Crosses You

3. _____
Above You

4. _____
Below You

5. _____
Behind You

6. _____
Before You

7. _____
You/the Querent

8. _____
Home, Family, Friends, and/or Environment

9. _____
Hopes and/or Fears

10. _____
Outcome or Culmination

Notes and/or Observations: (corresponding events, feelings, etc.)

II

SAMPLE READINGS FOR THE CELTIC CROSS SPREAD

or Burn an Orange Candle and Call Me in the Morning!

Burn an orange candle and call me in the morning! This is the advice the High Priestess of a Long Island Wiccan coven used to offer as a quick remedy to a stressful situation. A powerful healer, Irene was known for her infinite reserves of energy, her compassionate nature, and her great cooking. She also knew the color orange has a soothing effect by temporarily restoring balance and harmony.

So when Erica called me in the late evening, frantic and frustrated with her first attempt to give a Tarot card reading, I thought about recommending the High Priestess's *fix-all*. But I didn't want Erica to lose any sleep over this, like many beginners (including myself) have done. So I decided to *jump-start* her with an in-depth look as to how *I* might interpret this spread.

Erica was an aspiring dancer to whom I had given my crash course the previous evening. She appeared confident about what she had learned, but later, when she tried to give her sister a reading, she had trouble linking the cards together into a cohesive story.

Unfortunately this is very common because the mind tends to quickly slip back into rational mode. A rational mind is, of course, necessary to deal with day-to-day practicalities, but rational thinking interferes with Tarot card reading, which requires *non-thinking*. The mind must be trained to go into *intuitive* mode (that is, *non-thinking* mode). The spontaneity exercise helps to make this shift. That is why the fundamental teaching must be drilled into your head. People tend to forget it almost immediately and find themselves in a quandary. When beginning a Tarot reading, remember to always return to the basic instruction: *Look at the cards and say what you see.*

Because an in-depth analysis of a Tarot spread puts too much emphasis on *thinking*, it can be counter-productive. That is further evidenced by another trade secret: Adept readers are looking at the *overall picture(s)*; they are not breaking down the spread card-by-card, position-by-position. That would be an obstruction to the entire intuitive process.

Therefore this jump-start for Erica, along with two other samples, is included with great reluctance. *Please*, do not depend on these samples. The intention is only to give you an idea of *how* a spread *may* be interpreted by showing the basic mechanics of a reading. Peruse them once. Incorporate what you can readily comprehend. Skim over what does not immediately click. Then move forward; always continuing with the basic spontaneity practice: *Look at the cards and say what you see.*

Before we continue, there is one other issue. I have given permission to refer to the other sections, and, yes, that does include the section on *Possible Meanings*. I hope you did not peek into this section until after the basic instructions were faithfully followed. Even if you have (and I know many of you have, because that's human nature), I still encourage you to first *look at the cards and say what you see* before checking out my suggested meanings. Remember, I am teaching you how to depend on your own intuition to read Tarot cards and how to develop your own meanings. I don't want you to fall back into the aimless habit of looking up the meaning of each card. However, some people tell me reading the cards is easier for them knowing they have the option. But, when following these samples, try tuning in to your own intuition first. You will be amazed at the insights you get. And, don't be surprised if you totally disagree with my interpretations. That is an excellent sign of progress!

Referring to the dated worksheet Erica filled out [See Sample Celtic Cross Spread Worksheet (Erica)], lay your cards out accordingly. Now let's look at several detailed clues in this spread. Notice on the worksheet that key words or pithy meanings are given for each card. Relating to the spread before you and the notes on the worksheet, follow along, as I review the meanings of the positions step-by-step with the cards falling therein.

Erica chose the Queen of Pentacles as the significator for her sister. A very dark-haired woman, she is thirty-eight years old.

In Position 1, *This is what covers you.* This represents the atmosphere or *emotional* environment in which influences are working. Is there tension in the air? Is the atmosphere relaxed and easygoing? The 7 of Cups may indicate an atmosphere of fantasy, imagination, or delusion. The 5 of Wands could suggest that influences of manipulation, power plays, or mind games are operating in the atmosphere.

Look at the card that falls in Position 1, the 9 of Swords. *Say what you see.* Clearly this woman is worried and distraught. She sits up in bed, perhaps unable to sleep. This picture literally speaks for itself. Obviously, the *atmosphere* is filled with *worry*. *Worry* is a key word.

In Position 2, *This is what crosses you.* This can represent an obstacle or an aid. It depends on the card. Usually, if it is a positive card, it is helpful. If it is a negative card, it means there is an opposition, but not necessarily. At this point *intuitive* interpretation must be incorporated. Let's look at some possibilities.

Suppose it is the Queen of Wands. She may be a helpful woman. However, the Queen of Swords may be a jealous or difficult woman, an opposing force. That's an easy example.

Here is a more complicated example. Suppose Position 2 is a positive card, 3 of Cups (friends). However most of the other cards in the spread are difficult. The interpretation could very possibly go both ways. Friends could be helpful, or friends could be causing problems and interfering. Here again, your intuition must come into play; and, remember the cop's rule of thumb: *Your first hunch is usually your best*—and my rule of thumb, *spontaneity.* Go with the first thing that pops into your mind!

Most of the cards in this spread are positive. But a *spontaneous impression* to Justice is that this represents a lawyer or legal matter. Along with heightened intuition, life experience is another asset to deciphering Tarot cards, and *my* life experience

Sample Celtic Cross Spread Worksheet (Erica)

Date: 11/3/99

Significator Queen of Pentacles

1. 9 of Swords   worry
   What Covers You

2. Justice   lawyer
   What Crosses You

3. Strength   determination is needed
   Above You

4. The Magician   motivated by need for control and power
   Below You

5. 7 of Wands   power struggle
   Behind You

6. Wheel of Fortune   sudden luck or opportunity
   Before You

7. 4 of Cups   dreaming or wishing for something better
   You/The Querent

8. Knight of Cups   a message comes to the home
   Home, Family, Friends, and/or Environment

9. 5 of Pentacles   fear of financial problems
   Hopes and/or Fears

10. 8 of Pentacles   new job
    Outcome or Culmination

Notes and/or Observations: (corresponding events, feelings, etc.)
Wilma thought my sister would receive a lucky job offer.
11-8-99 my sister received a call at home about the offer.
She did not suffer any financial loss.

tells me that lawyers spell trouble. Furthermore, Justice is preceded by a difficult card. If it had been preceded by a positive card, The Star for instance, I might say it meant good news from a lawyer, a judge or about a legal matter.

Nevertheless, for practical purposes the key word need only be *lawyer*, and that is what is written on the worksheet. Eventually, as we proceed, the significance of Justice (in the context of the other cards) will become clear and the key word will make sense. This is another important lesson. Never belabor the meaning of a card. Keep moving along with the reading. Eventually everything will fall into place. This is a good example of how important spontaneity is. Stopping to think about *one* card will interfere with the psychic flow.

In Position 3, *This is above you.* This indicates what the querent is or should be aiming for in the matter. It is, many times, the solution to the issue or the answer to the problem.

Another interpretation is that this foretells what will happen in the future if no further action is taken. If it is a positive card, the querent is on the right path. If it is a negative card, the querent is moving in the wrong direction and should consider a change.

Again, this position is subject to interpretation depending on the card. These are merely guidelines designed to give you some focus. *Ultimately, the cards transcend the positions and your intuitive perception will transcend the cards.* A professional reader with a very large following told me how she *feels* the cards. And, that is exactly what you will soon notice you are *naturally* doing; when you *look at the cards and say what you see.* Keep this in mind as you go through these sample interpretations.

Regarding Position 3, the card of Strength speaks for itself. The querent should strive to be strong and determined in this situation. Note the pithy interpretation written on the worksheet, *determination is needed.*

In Position 4, *This is below you.* This describes the subconscious motivation of the querent or how the individual is thinking. A positive card indicates that one is spurred on by a confident prompting. A difficult card, let's say Knight of Swords, may mean the querent is motivated by a lot of anger. This position can also mean the underlying factor, basis, or foundation of the matter.

I would interpret The Magician in this position as the querent being *motivated by the need for control and power.*

In Position 5, *This is behind you.* This represents influences that are now passing away or the immediate past. However, from my experience, I have also seen this to indicate an influence from the distant past. There is a reason for this. When reading the Tarot, it is the subconscious mind of the querent that comes into play. If an issue from the long ago past is still having an emotional effect on the querent, even if not consciously, it may very well come out in the reading. In fact, you may see this happening with the *entire* spread, not only this position. What is on or in the querent's mind, consciously or unconsciously, comes out in the cards. This is a very curious phenomenon of psychic dynamics. I will address that in more detail in Chapter 3.

The 7 of Wands looks like a *power struggle* has recently taken place. Since it falls in the same spread with the card representing a lawyer, my immediate response would be that there is a connection. The reading is starting to make sense! Let's move on.

In Position 6, *This is before you.* This describes the future, what will be happening soon; or, it may reflect influences that have recently come into view. The Wheel of Fortune is without a doubt a positive card and in a propitious placement. It looks as if *sudden luck or opportunity* will be coming in very soon.

In Position 7, *This is you.* This signifies the querent and/or the querent's attitude in this situation. The 9 of Cups, the querent is happy or pleased. The 2 of Swords, the querent is uncertain or undecided. My spontaneous meaning to the card that falls here, the 4 of Cups, is *dreaming or wishing for something better.*

In Position 8, *This is your home, family, friends, and/or environment.* I usually interpret this position as representing the actual home, the family or family influences, friends, and/or, in a general sense, the actual *material* environment. The Empress in this position may mean a mother, a mother-type figure (a mother-in-law or aunt, for instance) or a mother-to-be (pregnant woman) comes to the home for a visit. The Knight of Cups, in this position, looks as if *a message comes to the home.*

In Position 9, *These are your hopes and/or fears.* Traditionally, this position is interpreted as the querent's hopes *or* fears relating to the issues at hand. However, I know one reader who interprets the hopes or fears as being one and the same. This adds a highly psychological slant to this interpretation. For example, one may be consciously hoping for success, yet unconsciously fearing it at the same time. Perhaps because of low self-esteem, one feels undeserving of success and is subconsciously more comfortable with failure. This complex interpretation is not necessary, but it is certainly *food for thought.* However, it may be easier to interpret this position as *either* hopes or fears, depending on the card. Here, the 5 of Pentacles, indicates to me there is a *fear of financial problems*.

In Position 10, *This is the outcome or culmination*. This tells how the situation will turn out in the end. Of course, a favorable card foretells a favorable conclusion. However, a negative card should not be construed as all is lost. Tarot devotees believe *the only thing constant in life is change*. If a difficult card falls in this position, look to Position 3 for a possible solution.

In this spread, the 8 of Pentacles shows a man working. My prediction would be a *new job*. However, more could be added to the interpretation of this position by combining its meaning with the card in Position 6, which indicates the future. In this spread, the Wheel of Fortune (sudden luck or opportunity) merged with the 8 of Pentacles (a new job) could be stretched to mean a *lucky new job opportunity*.

After reviewing the spread with Erica, I instructed her to link the key words together, and, while doing that, she would be creating a theme for the reading: *Worry* because of a *lawyer*; a recent *power struggle*; therefore, there is a *need for control*; *determination is needed* to resolve this issue; while *wishing for something better* or a better situation, but also afraid of having *financial problems*; a *message* is received bringing a *lucky opportunity* for *a new job*.

Instantaneously, Erica got an intuitive flash. There really was a theme because the cards were talking to her. Her sister, a legal secretary in a busy law firm, was having problems at work. There had been a severe power struggle with one particularly difficult lawyer. She needed a job where she had more control and had, in fact, applied for a job as an office manager. She wished very much to be hired for this job, since it appeared to be a more congenial situation. Meanwhile, however, she was so worried and distraught about the problems at the current job, she was afraid of being fired and losing wages. Hence, she actually had suffered several sleepless nights.

I told Erica *my* prediction was that her sister would indeed be hired for the job she wanted and would get a call at home in a few days. Erica noted this on the worksheet. A few days later, her sister was called at home and offered the job. Erica also noted the outcome of these turn of events on the worksheet. Once again I reminded Erica, as I am reminding you, to always refer back to the basic exercise: *Look at the cards and say what you see. A technical analysis of a spread is really not as important as making a connection with the cards themselves.* The next sample is an excellent example of this.

This spread was presented to me by Tina. A student at a college in Colorado, she was entering her sophomore year. Over the summer she had given this reading to her cousin's friend Brian. It is very significant because it shows how you can look at the overall spread and get an instant impression without going through it card-by-card. Remember the trade secret: *Professional readers are looking at the overall picture(s); they are not breaking down the spread card-by-card, position-by-position.*

Tina had been practicing diligently with the cards. She assured me she had followed my instructions to the *t*. However, when she gave this reading, something unusual happened. By following my instructions of *looking at the cards*, she suddenly got a rush of impressions. She felt *pulled in* by the cards, and noticed how intense and fixed her concentration was. Wisely, Tina relaxed, let the energy flow and followed her hunches. The impressions from the cards were so strong, she *naturally*, without even realizing it, began disregarding the positions in which they fell. Instead, she went on simply saying what she was seeing in the cards. It was as if she felt an invisible force leading her along. Tina called me for feedback and explained what she had done. Referring to the worksheet she filled out [See Sample Celtic Cross Spread Worksheet (Tina)], lay the cards out accordingly and follow along.

A quick overview of all the cards gave Tina some contradictory information. The Lovers crossed the querent. That should be good. But, the five difficult cards in the spread struck her as *not so good*. Tina's intuition told her something wasn't right. Her first insight was a love problem. But The World and The Sun also caught her eye. These spoke to her about travel to someplace warm and sunny. She then focused on the 4 of Swords and the 2 of Swords. These appeared to indicate sleeping on an issue (4 of Swords) and being torn apart (2 of Swords). The similarity between The Lovers and The Devil was another indicator. In The Devil, Tina saw a bad version of The Lovers. The Devil is followed by the 5 of Swords, a fight. And, the 8 of Swords looked like Brian may have felt a restriction.

Keep in mind, all of this information was rushing to Tina quickly. She really was, at that moment, *feeling* the cards, *not thinking* about them.

Tina decided to stick with the love theme, which *jumped* right at her. The second theme that hit her was the travel theme, and there was no denying anxiety and stress were visible in the cards. Tying all this to The Chariot, Tina felt that Brian wanted to get moving on something.

Here's her interpretation. Brian felt restricted and torn apart in a relationship. He was trying to sort it out. There was a nasty argument with a love interest. He was very angry. He really wanted freedom (The Fool). Tina concluded that in the future

Sample Celtic Cross Spread Worksheet (Tina)

Date: July 9, 2000

Significator Knight of Wands

1. The Chariot   wants to get moving
   What Covers You

2. The Lovers   a love issue
   What Crosses You

3. 4 of Swords   sleeping on an issue
   Above You

4. 2 of Swords   torn apart
   Below You

5. 8 of Swords   restrictions
   Behind You

6. The Sun   a sunny climate
   Before You

7. The Devil   a bad relationship
   You/The Querent

8. 5 of Swords   an argument
   Home, Family, Friends, and/or Environment

9. The Fool   freedom
   Hopes and/or Fears

10. The World   travel
    Outcome or Culmination

Notes and/or Observations: (corresponding events, feelings, etc.)

Brian had doubts about a restricting relationship. He and his
girlfriend had an argument and broke up. Brian was headed for
the West Coast.

he was going to travel to a warm and sunny climate, perhaps California. Tina couldn't figure out what travel had to do with the love problem. But she followed her spontaneous feelings.

Brian confirmed the reading. He told Tina he wanted adventure, and had been thinking about traveling to California. But his girlfriend wanted to stay on the East Coast. He began to feel restricted in this relationship, and couldn't decide what to do. Then they had a huge argument. That made his decision for him. He broke off the relationship and was en route to the West Coast.

Tina was uncomfortable about how she had done this. It certainly was an unfamiliar feeling. But I explained to her that, regardless of how it felt, it was correct. She had really given a *psychic* Tarot card reading! This is what happens when you go for the overall picture(s). You begin to *feel* the cards, and they convey their messages to you on a subconscious level.

Tina had learned a very important lesson. There really are no formulas for reading Tarot cards. There are guidelines; your *feelings*, however, are going to be your strongest guide. Reading Tarot cards is an intuitive art, not a mathematical equation. Remember, when you *look at the cards*, you are getting a *feeling* instantly. The images evoke a response in the subconscious mind. There is a *spontaneous reaction*. That is why I encourage you to immediately *say what you see*.

Another aspect Tina learned was that of fixed concentration. Tina felt as if the cards were pulling her in. This is what happens when you are making a psychic connection with the cards; and it is easily accomplished by simply *looking at the cards*. You will probably be aware of this even in the initial learning stages. Stay connected and go with the flow.

In Chapter 3 under the question, *How exactly do Tarot cards work?*, I write about how the cards serve as a focusing tool for harnessing psychic energy. After reading Tarot cards for so many years, I am able to focus as soon as the first card is placed down. I immediately go with my feelings; and, therefore, I instantly lock into *psychic mode*. I keep this focus as I quickly lay the cards out. The ability to focus instantly is a key to giving a *psychic* Tarot reading. Liken this to threading a needle. That is the hard part. However, once the needle is threaded, the sewing is easy. It's the same thing when making a psychic connection with the Tarot cards. You are threading the *psychic* needle. Once the connection is made, the reading is easy. Tina is definitely on the right track!

Other interpretations could be drawn from this spread. And they'd all be accurate. That's what is so intriguing about these cards. It's what you, the reader, see in them. That is why I instruct you to *look at the cards and say what you see*.

This is another *sample example*. This reading was given by Brendan, a web site designer, to his mother. Brendan confessed he had glanced at the section on *Possible Meanings* before finishing the instructions in *The First 2 Hours*. However, he had *still* taken the time to learn the basic technique of looking at the cards. So I forgave him for this indiscretion. He also told me that he disagreed with many of my interpretations and had quickly come up with some of his own meanings. That is highly acceptable and his reading was highly accurate. Refer to his worksheet, and lay the cards out accordingly. Then follow along as Brendan explained his on-target interpretation.

Significator—Queen of Wands: Brendan saw his mother as an industrious entrepreneur.

Position 1—10 of Wands: Brendan's mother was overwhelmed with responsibility. This is a matter of which Brendan was already aware.

Position 2—The Empress: Brendan's mother was taking care of *her* mother, Brendan's grandmother, who had been very ill. Brendan knew this, too. It played into the overwhelming responsibility put upon his mother.

Position 3—2 of Cups: Brendan's parents had divorced two years ago. His mother was seeing a man who wanted to marry her, but she felt she wasn't ready yet. Based on the card, Brendan could see that this relationship did make his mother happy. He also suggested that marriage would be a good move for her.

Position 4—The Hanged Man: Brendan's mother was giving up a lot of her time to care for his grandmother. Until the reading, Brendan had not been aware of how much his mother had really been sacrificing for the care of her own mother. This is something Brendan's mother kept to herself. Here, the reading was revealing unknown information.

Position 5—The Knight of Swords: One week ago, his mother's car had broken down.

Position 6—9 of Pentacles: Brendan's mother was a *shopaholic*. She firmly believed *when the going gets tough, the tough go shopping*. Brendan predicted a shopping spree coming up soon.

Position 7—5 of Wands: Brendan predicted his mother would be starting an exercise program, something she had never before done. She admitted to looking into gyms and exercise studios. This was a very big piece of surprise information from the reading. But Brendan had followed the *golden rule* and read what he saw in the card, and by doing so he learned a valuable lesson. You never know what you will see in the cards

Sample Celtic Cross Spread Worksheet (Brendan)

Date: 1/28/02

Significator Queen of Wands

1. 10 of Wands   Mom is overwhelmed with responsibility
   What Covers You

2. The Empress   Mom is taking care of grandmom
   What Crosses You

3. 2 of cups   Mom should get married again
   Above You

4. The Hanged Man   a sacrifice
   Below You

5. Knight of Swords   a car problem
   Behind You

6. 9 of Pentacles   a shopping spree
   Before You

7. 5 of Wands   working out/exercise
   You/The Querent

8. Page of Swords   Julie is in the home
   Home, Family, Friends, and/or Environment

9. 5 of Pentacles   money worries
   Hopes and/or Fears

10. Queen of Cups   a new hair style
    Outcome or Culmination

Notes and/or Observations: (corresponding events, feelings, etc.)

Mom bought some new clothes, got a hair cut and makeover, dyed hair blond, and joined a gym.

when giving someone else a reading. Do not presume you already know what is going on in that person's life. You really don't. That is why it is important to *look at the cards and say what you see*, not what you *think* can or cannot happen.

Position 8—Page of Swords: Brendan saw this card as his younger sister, Julie, who had been living in an apartment near the local college she attended. Impulsive and temperamental, Julie was a handful. His mother had been relieved when Julie moved out. But now Brendan saw Julie in his mother's home. How could that be? Here again, Brendan went with what he saw in the cards. His mother then informed him with dismay that Julie was moving back home. Another unexpected revelation from the cards!

Position 9—5 of Pentacles: His mother was worried about money. This made sense. His ailing grandmother and the cost of repairing the car was causing understandable financial distress.

Position 10—Queen of Cups: Brendan predicted along with his mother's imminent shopping spree that she would get a new hairstyle and makeover. His mother confirmed; she had been thinking of doing that, too.

Brendan gave his mother a great reading. He looked at the cards, followed his intuition, and, despite my admonishment, got a bit of a boost by looking up some of the meanings. All that matters is the end result. It worked.

And if these sample readings don't work for you, burn an orange candle and *e-mail* me in the morning! My e-mail address is provided at the end of Chapter 3.

III

ARE WE HAVING FUN YET?

QUESTIONS, ANSWERS, TROUBLESHOOTING, AND FINETUNING

Janet was terrified. It was midnight when she called. She was scared to death!

Having graduated from college two years ago, she had a great job at an Internet company and appreciated the security of a steady paycheck. But Janet passionately wanted to pursue a career in acting, and was torn between practicality and starry-eyed ambitions. Meanwhile she channeled her creative energies into studying the Tarot.

She whispered in a fearful voice: *"Why does the Death card keep coming up in my practice readings?"*

No need for alarm, I assured her. It is a very curious and common phenomenon that many people experience during the early phases of working with Tarot cards. While practicing on yourself, in many of these spreads, the Death card will keep appearing over and over again. I remember this happening to me countless times; and, since it was often late at night, I was spooked! But the Death card is really considered a *positive* card; and, I believe its frequent appearance in these initial practice readings also has quite positive indications.

Let's take a close look at the Death card. Pull it out of the deck. *Look at the card and say what you see.* A skeleton rides on a *white* horse. He is greeted by an official-looking man (a priest or bishop, perhaps) bearing *gifts*. The *sun rises* in the background.

These elements of the symbolism can be construed as auspicious, intending to convey a *spiritual* connotation. It is the name of the card, *Death*, that terrifies people. But since the symbolism has a spiritual implication, this Tarot card bespeaks of a *spiritual death* and that tends to play out as a psychological transformation.

A spiritual death is really a rebirth or an awakening to a new consciousness or awareness. However it requires a *letting-go* or a releasing of that which no longer works in our lives and impedes our growth; and that is the death (figuratively speaking) of the old, the worn out, and the useless. In order to move forward we must let go of what is no longer needed in our lives; we must clear away all the debris. To use a common expression, we must *cut off the dead wood*.

Fear of death, that is the actual death of the physical body, comes from the uncertainty about where we will go after death. Therefore, the notion of a *spiritual* death evokes the exact same fear; and this fear plays out in many aspects of our lives. Thus we hold on to many unnecessary things in our lives because of the fear of what life would be like without them. We tell ourselves we need these things for our survival; that our survival depends on keeping those things in our lives which should really be discarded. Because of our fear of *the unknown*, we convince ourselves we cannot live without that which has grown obsolete.

Think about all the decaying things in your life that you clung to while all the time believing that your life would be incomplete without them: friends (you may have outgrown), a (bad) love relationship or a (bad) marriage, a job, rigid political or religious beliefs, even hobbies or interests. Eventually and reluctantly you had to let go of them. Perhaps you, yourself, finally realized it. Or perhaps they were even taken from you. Regardless of the circumstances, the process of letting go could have been frightening because there was an uncertainty about what would happen or what life would be like without them. This is why even a *spiritual death* can be quite difficult.

But once there is a release, the way is cleared for newness to enter your life. Many people report feeling light and free once the unnecessary has been released. That is why people who go through a religious transformation say they have been *reborn*. A spiritual death, which is really a *spiritual rebirth*, is a renewal. With a spiritual rebirth comes an awakening, a whole new consciousness, a new awareness, an enlightenment.

So the Death card is not the card of physical death; but rather it symbolizes the death of the old, the worn-out, or the useless. Look closely at the card again. A *white* horse; white is the color of spiritual purity and innocence. The *rising* (not *setting*) sun tells of a new dawning day, bringing with it new beginnings, new directions, a whole new cycle of one's life. Although the letting-go may have been uncomfortable, the way now becomes cleared for new opportunities to enter our lives. *When a door closes, a window opens.*

The Tarot opens the gate to new spiritual horizons. When

you begin working with the Tarot, your intuition begins to develop; and, along with that, you will begin to experience a new *spiritual* awareness or consciousness. This moves you into a new cycle of your life. Hence, the Death card, symbolizing this new consciousness and moving into a new cycle of your life, may frequently pop up in these very first practice readings.

The thirteenth card of the Tarot deck is a powerful card that imparts a profound esoteric insight through its symbolism: *Out with the old and in with the new.*

How should I read inverted/reversed upside down cards? All the standard books give two meanings for each card. One meaning, if the card falls right-side-up; another, if the card falls upside down. The reversed meanings are negative. You are then instructed to memorize *both* of these meanings. However, remember my way of doing things does not involve memorizing meanings. So when it comes to reversed cards I, as well as many other professional readers I know, do not read them any differently! I have two reasons for this.

First: Trying to interpret a card by giving it a reversed meaning forces you to pause and think, and that interferes with spontaneity and the flow of psychic impressions. Remember the professional reader who told me, she *feels* the cards? You cannot feel the cards if you are trying to think about a meaning.

Second: There are already difficult cards in the deck that can indicate severe challenges. For example, the suit of Swords, The Tower, and The Devil. I, therefore, see no necessity for interpreting cards in a reversed manner (with a negative meaning) if there are already cards to indicate negative influences. Suppose the 10 of Swords is reversed? Some people think this is the *worst* card in the deck. How can you make the interpreta-tion of the *worst* card *worse*? My opinion is that the negative cards speak for themselves by turning up in the spread, regard-less of the way they fall.

Again you are going to have to decide for yourself how you want to deal with this. Your personal style! Tarot card reading is an art; you are now the artist. But I think trying to interpret re-versed cards differently will cause confusion. I can assure you as long as you continue with the basic exercise: *Look at the cards and say what you see*, each card will talk to you any which way it falls.

Why is the querent supposed to cut the deck with the left hand? This is a ritual that I believe to be nothing more than a Gypsy superstition. Esoterically speaking, the unconscious mind is symbolized by the left hand, while the conscious mind is symbolized by the right hand. This distinction is clearly ap-plied to palm reading. The left hand tells what the individual is born with (the unconscious mind). The right hand tells what one will (consciously) do with these inherent qualities. Hence, logistically, the left hand is the passive hand and the right hand is the dominant active hand. (Of course, this is reversed if someone is left-handed.) So I assume, since a Tarot card read-ing involves connecting with the subconscious mind, this most likely explains the origin of this ritual.

While it does serve to set the mystical tone associated with a Tarot card reading, there is no magical power afforded by this observance. If the querent accidentally uses the right hand to cut or even cuts the deck to the right instead of the left, it will not affect the reading in any way. I have seen this happen many times, when I am giving a reading. It is, in my opinion, no big deal. And since, according to metaphysicians, *nothing ever happens by accident*, I think maybe there is a reason for this minor error. Remember the Tarot is an intuitive medium and it is using the intuition that gives good results.

Although I overlook a mistake in the cutting of the deck, I might add there are two things I do insist on. One is that the cards are cut into *three* piles. Not two, not four, but three piles exactly. And after the deck has been cut, I insist that the querent does not touch them for any reason. *I* am the one who picks them up. I realize there is no magic involved here either, but it's *my* personal style!

What if the querent is left-handed? There are those who say if the querent is left-handed, the cut should be made with the right hand and the reader should pick up the cards with the left hand. In other words, the entire ritual should be reversed. Personally I find this to be too confusing and cumbersome to deal with. I like things to be simple. I believe simplicity will facilitate the flow of positive energy and intuition. So I keep the ritual the same, regardless of whether or not someone is right- or left-handed. Again what you do is your decision. *Your* personal style.

What do you mean when you say, "Shuffle the cards until they feel right"? The shuffling, in general, gives the querent an opportunity to develop a rapport with the cards and to put her personal *vibrations* into them. By asking the querent to shuffle the cards until they *feel right*, you are further encouraging her to focus on the cards and to make a connection with them on a *feeling* or *vibrational* level. This makes it easier for the reader to intuitively tune in to the querent (as well as the cards) and give a more effective reading. When giving a Tarot reading, you are working with energies and vibrations. So a mutual tune-in by both the querent and the reader greatly facilitates the flow of psychic energy.

Is it true that some readers will not allow anyone else to touch their cards? I have heard this, but never seen it. Rumor has it there are some readers who will not allow anyone else to touch their cards in an attempt to keep them totally free of negative vibrations. Instead of having the querent shuffle the cards, the Tarot reader will shuffle the cards and *concentrate* on the querent. If the reader's concentration is good, the results will be also.

In some instances, if a reader feels that someone who has come for a consultation is emitting negative energy, the reader may, in that case, choose not to let the querent handle her cards in order to protect them.

I have always viewed my cards as *user-friendly*. In fact, I rather *like* the querent putting her vibrations into my cards. It helps me with the tune-in. Here again, this is going to be your personal choice. Experiment to see what works for you.

If at any time you feel your cards are overly saturated with unwanted vibes, you can cleanse them by passing them through incense smoke. A classic occult formula is the combination of frankincense and asafoetida. Frankincense is for *purifying* negative energies. It has a pleasant aroma. Asafoetida is for *cleansing* negative energies. It is malodorous! Together the odor is potent. You'll have to look for these in a specialty shop, and they must be burned on a small piece of a special type of charcoal and in an incense burner. A specialty shop will be able to provide you with all the necessary equipment. However, you really need not go to such an extreme. Any standard joss stick incense will do the job quite effectively.

Do Tarot cards require special care? Tarot cards should be accorded the same care and respect given to any sacred object or prayer book. Traditionally they are supposed to be wrapped in silk and stored in a wooden box that is placed high on a shelf.

Silk insulates against unwanted *spiritual* vibrations. The customary colors for the silk cloth are either black or purple. Unfortunately, black has gotten a bad rap and is often associated with evil or the *black arts*. This is an unfounded misconception because black is really a very spiritual color. Members of the clergy such as priests, monks, and nuns wear black. As for purple, it has always been associated with spirituality and used ecclesiastically.

The wooden box protects against undesirable *earthly* vibrations. By placing the box high on a shelf, it is symbolic of heavenly elevation.

I believe, however, that you can store Tarot cards any way you want as long as you care for them with reverence. I keep one deck wrapped in a red satin scarf and secured in a wooden box bearing a carving of an owl (a wise old owl); and another deck wrapped in a cloth scarf that has a very special meaning to me.

It is also customary to spread the silk cloth on the table and place the cards on it when giving the reading. Although this is another practice I, personally, have never felt to be necessary, you can incorporate this aspect in accordance with your own individual taste.

Should I sleep with Tarot cards under my pillow? This is another traditional suggestion I have read about, and was also recommended to me by a friend many years ago. Theoretically this may bridge a link between the cards and the deep subconscious mind.

My friend told me of a bizarre experience she had one night. Routinely in the habit of spreading the cards out under her pillow while sleeping, she had disturbing nightmares one particular night. She awoke to find The Devil had surfaced to the top!

I tried this practice myself. But, since I am such a restless sleeper, the cards did nothing more than get in the way of my constant tossing and turning. Hence I made no more attempts at this uncomfortable experiment.

You might try selecting only one card that you especially like and sleeping on that to see what happens. This is another procedure you will have to test for yourself.

What is the Tarot (or Tarot cards)? The Tarot, pronounced *tarō*, is a deck of seventy-eight cards containing symbols from many ancient cultures. Today it is commonly used for divination or fortune-telling.

The deck is divided into two parts: the Major Arcana (or Major Trumps) and the Minor Arcana (or Minor Trumps). The Major Arcana consists of twenty-two cards. The remaining fifty-six cards make up the Minor Arcana, which is divided into four suits: Pentacles, Cups, Wands, and Swords. These suits correspond to the four elements—earth, water, fire, and air—which the ancients believed made up the world. Each suit has an ace, king, queen, knight, and page as well as numbered cards from two to ten.

Where do Tarot cards come from? The history of the Tarot is vague and unclear. There are countless theories; and for every one theory there are at least two counter-theories disproving it.

Some sources say Tarot cards originated in China, others say Egypt, and still others say their roots are in India. Yet the first clear historical references say the cards appeared in Europe around the fourteenth century as a game known as Tarrochi. It is ironically this classical deck that has remained relatively unchanged for more than six hundred years!

Most likely the Major Arcana began developing first and gradually evolved over a period of centuries into the twenty-two Major Trumps. One popular theory is that they might be the very earliest recordings of myths, fables, and significant historical events. In the beginnings of civilization, these accounts were handed down orally, but eventually they were put into pictorial form.

Indeed many of these Major Trumps are clearly reminiscent of biblical stories. For instance The Lovers appears to me to be the depiction of the story of Adam and Eve; The Tower, an obvious illustration of the Tower of Babel; and The Hanged Man is suggestive of the crucifixion.

The Hermit reminds me of Diogenes, the Greek philosopher and ascetic, who is thought to have lived from roughly 412 B.C. to 323 B.C. Diogenes is the subject of numerous apocryphal stories. His endless search for an honest man was supposedly conducted in broad daylight with a *lighted* lantern! Note the uncanny resemblance of that legendary image to the card itself.

Another popular theory about the Major Arcana tells of the spiritual leaders of many countries and cultures gathering together in Fez (once a province of Morocco) around the year

1200, sometime after the great library at Alexandria in Egypt was destroyed. Their objective was to preserve esoteric teachings, but in order to do so they had to bridge the language barrier. Since in ancient times most people did not read or write, symbols were used instead of words to convey information. Thus a common language of symbols (based on mystical symbols taken from many cultures) was developed and put onto cards; while the key was to remain a secret knowledge that was exclusively transmitted by word of mouth from one generation to the next.

There has always been speculation that the Gypsies brought the cards into Europe. Here is a perfect example of an espoused theory with a valid counter-theory disproving it. In this instance, historical fact easily proves the cards were in Europe before the Gypsies, who may have arrived around the late fourteenth century or early fifteenth century. However, the Gypsies probably were the first to start using them for divination in order to earn their livings.

It wasn't until the eighteenth century that a French writer, Antoine Court de Gébelin, noted the cards' mystical symbology. Soon after he wrote about it, many other occult writers followed suit and began touting the immense repository of esoteric knowledge contained in the imagery.

It is said that the symbolism in Tarot cards contains hidden truths about the fundamental laws of the universe and the mysterious wisdom found in the forces underlying the cosmos. The pictorial representations illustrate the steps of the soul's progression through spiritual growth. As consciousness unfolds, the Tarot subtly discloses its secrets.

Often described as the *ultimate Rorschach test*, what we see in the cards is merely a reflection of our own inner psyches.

Therefore by using the Tarot in a practical manner, as a tool for fortune-telling, the subconscious mind easily connects on an intuitive level with the cards' enlightening doctrine.

Is there any connection between Tarot cards and playing cards? The structure of playing cards is very similar to that of Tarot cards, except that playing cards do not have a knight, and a jack takes the place of a page. The suits of playing cards—diamonds, hearts, clubs, and spades—correspond with the Tarot suits of Pentacles, Cups, Wands, and Swords respectively; and, the playing cards' joker is an obvious offshoot of the Tarot cards' Fool (or vice versa).

As for the history of playing cards, it is equally as vague as that of Tarot cards. Some historians think that playing cards may have come from China or Korea. At some point they were combined with the Major Arcana and fashioned into the Tarrochi deck.

However other scholars believe that playing cards are actually the offspring of the original seventy-eight Tarot cards. Thus the age-old question *"Which came first: the chicken or the egg?"* remains unanswered.

What is the difference between the Major Arcana and the Minor Arcana? It is said that the Major Arcana deals with spiritual or psychological changes or *internal* conflicts, while the Minor Arcana is indicative of daily activities, mundane events, external influences, and/or people.

However, my experience has been that these distinctions can be interpreted interchangeably. I have seen the Major Arcana represent people and outside influences, and I have seen the Minor Arcana indicate internal psychological changes.

The interpretations are always ultimately subject to the intuition of the reader.

What do the four suits of the Tarot mean? Traditionally, Pentacles indicate issues dealing with money, business, and financial and material matters. Cups represent issues of love, romance, friendship, happiness, emotion, and relationships. Wands signify dynamic energy, enterprise, creation, agriculture, and work. Swords are interpreted as aggression, strife, stress, tension, and sometimes violence.

For easy reference:

Pentacles	(Diamonds)	Earth	Money
Cups	(Hearts)	Water	Love
Wands	(Clubs)	Fire	Work
Swords	(Spades)	Air	Strife

Should the querent concentrate on a specific question when shuffling? There are some Tarot writers who give this as a standard recommendation. The querent is asked to concentrate on or hold a specific question in mind when shuffling the cards. However I have always found it more effective to follow a different procedure.

First, I ask the querent to clear her mind. When one is relaxed, energies tend to flow more smoothly. If one is anxious, energies can bottle up. Thinking too hard about a specific question may create interfering tensions. If I sense the querent is too nervous, I suggest she take a few deep breaths before I begin dealing out the cards.

By the way, if nervousness and tension are too great, I may not even continue with the reading because the anxieties would produce a great barrier. I therefore ask the querent to reschedule the appointment. I know several other successful professionals who follow this practice also.

Assuming the emotional state of the querent is conducive to giving a reading, I prefer to initially see what comes out. (Several of my colleagues also agree with this course, I might add.) So I begin by throwing one to three different spreads. Many times the answer to the question the querent is looking for comes out then. And, since it is a spontaneous response, unfettered by any preprogrammed thinking on my part as a reader, it is usually quite an accurate psychic insight.

Besides, life's issues are sometimes so complex that there could be many conditions affecting the querent's concern that aren't even realized. By giving an impartial answer, many of these other factors can be intuitively picked up, too.

So my first recommendation is to candidly see what comes out. However, there are advanced spreads in Chapter 5 that can be used to answer a specific question. Or you can even use the basic Celtic Cross Spread for a specific question. These are some more things you are going to have to experiment with yourself, to see what works. No matter which spreads you use, you will get insightful information as long as you *look at the cards and say what you see.*

Can a *yes* or *no* question be answered with the Tarot? There are spreads in Chapter 5 that can be used to answer a *yes* or *no* question. Again, because there are so many complex factors entering into a particular situation, and because life's issues are rarely clear, cut-and-dry, I do not always find these spreads to be effective, particularly, as I have mentioned, when there is a strong emotional investment in a given matter.

There are times when the cards will not directly answer the question being asked, but instead will give an indirect answer because there are *unknown* influences affecting the issue. It is still important to take note of the cards appearing in the spread because *messages are always coming through*, even if it is not one you are looking for.

Some of my colleagues have reported remarkable success using Tarot cards to answer *yes* or *no* questions. This is something else you will have to experiment with to see what works for you.

One piece of advice: If you try these spreads, *the clearer the question, the clearer the answer.* A muddled question yields a muddled answer. Try to phrase the question succinctly in eight words or less, and ask the cards only one question at a time. By the way, the question can be asked verbally (out loud), or the querent can silently think about it to herself.

Can all questions be answered with the Tarot? The late Eden Gray, one of the foremost Tarot authorities of the twentieth century, maintained that *any* question could be answered with Tarot cards and insisted on their "unfailing accuracy." Lynn M. Buess in his book, *The Tarot and Transformation*, agrees. "A Tarot reading can be extraordinarily accurate and detailed," writes Buess. But, he goes on to write, "There are times, however, when a reading is general, garbled and seems extremely confusing." My experience is consistent with Buess's findings. At times, a reading is unbelievably lucid, but clarity is not the case with every reading. And, after nearly four decades of peering into the future, I have come to the conclusion that with any form of divination, there are infinite possibilities as well as frustrating limitations.

I have previously mentioned the overwhelming influence of

the emotional state of the querent. If the querent is anxious or has a strong emotional investment in a matter, the clarity of the reading will be greatly affected. And this is what factors into the greatest and most frustrating limitation with Tarot cards.

Dion Fortune writes in *Practical Occultism in Daily Life*: "Anyone with practical experience of seership knows that to try to obtain enlightenment by psychic means concerning any matter in which one has a strong emotional bias is seldom satisfactory, for the bias vitiates the results to such a degree that they may prove most misleading . . . for the strong emotion in the mind of the querent is very apt to influence the psychic unconsciously, so that the results obtained may either be colored by desire, or, if the influence is unconsciously resisted, may lean to the other extreme." This kind of confusion is most noticeably evident with romantic issues!

Some of the most amazing insights I have had with the cards have been while reading at parties and special events. Perhaps it is because the guests are not looking for anything in particular and are completely relaxed. This is quite the contrary, when someone comes in for a private consultation. At that time, there is usually a high level of anticipation.

But you have asked me about *any* question; to which I answer, *not everything* is given to us. After all, we are only humans; and perhaps not supposed to know everything. By *divining* we are trying to intercept the *Universal Mind*, and this is not as easy as it seems. Cosmic tools, such as Tarot cards, astrology, numerology, and palmistry, give us a connection between time and space and provide us with enormous amounts of information. But, there are some things that are not in our hands and are none of our business. Case in point, questions about death or illness. These are strictly *verboten*!

If ever I am asked when someone will die, my answer is, "Only God knows that." I also avoid diagnostic questions about health because I think it is irresponsible and unethical for a psychic to answer them. My response is, "I'm not a doctor."

However sometimes certain taboo topics do come out unexpectedly—especially when no one is looking for them! This anomaly supports the theory of emotional investment. I talk about this in Chapter 6, along with an unusual question I was asked to answer with Tarot cards when appearing on *Live With Regis* on Halloween of 2000. Regis asked me, "Who would win the presidential election?" It was an odd question to ask with the Tarot but the cards came through, proving that the possibilities can be infinite.

Regardless of the questions you ask or the spreads you use, keep in mind the true purpose of divination as described by Dion Fortune: "A divination should be regarded as a weather-vane which shows which way the winds of the invisible forces are blowing; but it should always be remembered that a weather-vane is not meant to determine the course that a ship is to take; it merely indicates how best to trim the sails."

Is there a way to time events with Tarot cards? One of the difficulties encountered with Tarot cards and other forms of *psychic* divination is the timing of events. When reading the Tarot, we tune into the astral level. This is a higher dimensional plane commonly known as the *fourth dimension*. According to Swami Vishnudevananda, in his book *The Complete Illustrated Book of Yoga*, "all extrasensory perception and these so-called unexplained mysteries are the functions of the astral body in a higher dimensional place." Time and space (as we perceive it) are transcended on the astral level, making it difficult to determine the timing of events.

Many old-time readers used to say an event will take place in three days, three weeks, or three months because of the impossibility of psychically zeroing in on timing. In fact, there is a very old psychic joke: *Leave the timing to George. George* was a make-believe character invented by old occultists. Since they couldn't deal with timing, they used to say *George* would take care of it.

However, here are some technical guidelines that you may find helpful. Use them in conjunction with your intuition. But keep in mind that these guidelines are not laws. So you can be flexible with them.

▪ The four suits of the Tarot can represent measures of time: Pentacles—years; Cups—days or weeks; Wands—months; Swords—hours or days.

▪ The Ace of Pentacles could be interpreted as approximately one year; the Ace of Wands, one month; the Ace of Cups, one day or one week; the Ace of Swords, one hour or one day.

▪ The Major Trump cards usually indicate an event or situation taking place immediately.

▪ The Minor Trumps may represent less immediate events or events further into the future.

▪ Many modern readers, myself included, can be more precise with timing by using a combination of astrology and numerology. These are more grounded esoteric sciences and I have excellent results with this blend.

With astrology, the phases of the moon are very important. Observation of these lunar phases can be easily incorporated into your readings. (Most standard calendars indicate the lunar phases.)

■ The new moon is the time for new beginnings. It produces a new cycle. Many issues are triggered off with the new moon; new developments come into view or new matters come up. It is the time seeds are planted, projects are initiated, or something is started.

■ The full moon brings matters to culmination, completion or fruition. It is the time of endings. Look to the full moon to mark the finality of an issue or when, in fact, the querent will find an answer to the matter, or something unexpectedly surfaces.

While on the subject of the full moon, here is an interesting bit of information. The full moon is a very emotional time. As the moon gets bigger, people's problems get bigger. Issues become magnified and exaggerated and people *have* to find answers. Many readers notice more calls for consultations around this time!

The full moon is also said to be a very psychic time! I have had extraordinary discernments when reading at this time, but have not noticed the same with the new moon, except on a solar eclipse, which is a new moon eclipse.

Some people recommend giving readings only when the

moon is in a water sign, especially Pisces. (An astrological ephemeris or astrological calendar provides this data.) Water is the psychic element.

But I have noticed that regardless of the sign or phases of the moon, extraordinary insights can still be had. The internal condition of the querent seems to be weightier than external celestial influences.

With numerology, it is helpful to know the querent's personal year, personal month, and personal day. Numerology is a valuable shortcut to timing.

Here is an example of how I combined my knowledge of astrology and numerology in order to zero in on a time frame when reading for a businessman. From the cards I could tell he was waiting for a phone call about a new business venture. The Ace of Cups, 10 of Pentacles, and The Chariot were some of the cards that came up in the Celtic Cross Spread. He was in a *1* personal year and a *1* personal month—a time of new beginnings. I predicted he would get a call with good news on the day of the full moon, which was in five days and fell exactly on his *1* personal day. Sure enough, the following week, his wife phoned to tell me the call came exactly when I had predicted.

Again I want to remind you that these guidelines are not written in stone. These are merely some additional tools you may find useful. You are going to have to experiment with them. Be sure to take *dated* notes and follow up on what happens.

Can the numbers on the Tarot cards be used for timing? With the Major Trumps, I have never found this to be effective. Nor have I found it effective to interpret the *meanings* of the individual Major Trump cards in the context of their respective numbers, because to me they never fit, especially with the traditional numerology I studied. Others disagree with me and think *most*, but *not all*, of these numbers fit nicely, with this discrepancy due to the fact that we are not even certain of the original arrangement of the Major Arcana.

With the four suits of the Minor Arcana, I have been able to incorporate the number on a card with a measure of time corresponding to that suit and had good results. For example, the 2 of Swords may be interpreted as an event that will take place in two hours or two days; 4 of Wands, four months; 6 of Cups, six days or six weeks. Here again, there is a lot of intuitive feeling. This is something else you'll have to play around with, perhaps while also working in the querent's personal numerological vibes.

Can you give me a crash course in basic numerology? Numerology is basic mathematics. Grab a pencil and paper. In no time you will be doing the calculations in your head. Follow along!

Start by calculating the *universal year*. Add the four digits of the current year 2004. 2 + 0 + 0 + 4 = 6. 2004 is a 6 *universal year. Always reduce to a single digit.* If this had been 1997, the procedure would have been as follows: 1 + 9 + 9 + 7 = 26. But in numerology everything must be re-added in order to be reduced to a single digit. So 2 + 6 = 8. The year 1997 was an 8 *universal year.*

To find your *personal year vibration*, add your *birth month* and *birth day* to the current *universal year* (which is 2004 or a 6). If your birthday is January 17 (1/17), add 1 + 1 + 7 + 6 = 15. Remember to *always reduce to a single digit*: 1 + 5 = 6. Your *personal year* for 2004 is a 6. (Remember to recalculate this for next year, 2005.)

To find your *personal month vibration*, add your *personal year* to the current *calendar month*. Let's say it's August (8). If your *personal year* is a 6, add 6 + 8 = 14. Remember to *always reduce to a single digit* (if necessary): 1 + 4 = 5. Your *personal month* is a 5.

To find your *personal day vibration*, add your *personal month* to the current *calendar day*. Let's say it's the fifth day (5) of the month. If your *personal month* is a 5, add 5 + 5 = 10. *Always reduce to a single digit.* 1 + 0 = 1. Your *personal day* (for August 5, 2004) is a 1.

It's so easy, a monkey can do it!

The vibration of the personal year has the strongest influence on our lives and is in effect for the entire *calendar* year. For instance, if you are in an 8 personal year during 2004, this vibration will be felt from the beginning of January 2004 to the end of December 2004.

The personal year vibration indicates when to expect major life-altering changes; when to make life's *important* changes and serious decisions; when to plan and time *major* life altering activities; what kinds of experiences to expect; what kinds of opportunities may present themselves and which types of pursuits are best started or avoided.

The vibration of the personal months and personal days give us the same information as the personal years but their influence does not have a broad life-changing impact. The personal months and personal days are useful for zeroing in on the precise timing, specific planning and scheduling of activities.

Now for the key to the interpretations.

1—This is a time of new beginnings. Start a new job, new career, new business or project. Many people move to a new location in a 1 personal year. Do something original. Get out and meet new people or expect new people to come into your life, exposing you to new ideas. Be aggressive and go after what you want. Be your own boss and do it your way. This is a time of independence and a very active and busy time. Because your independent and pioneering spirit strongly prevails, this is not the best time to start a new relationship. It is not the worst time for marriage, however, but you may be too focused on yourself to make the necessary compromises. Sometimes in a 1 personal year a marriage is entered into out of boredom or the need to do something new. However, a 1 personal day is great for a *first* date.

2—This is the time to be passive and patient. Take the back seat. Follow, do not lead. Be diplomatic, cooperative, and agreeable. Become a collector. Take care of details. Join groups, clubs, teams, or organizations. In your 1 personal year seeds were planted and projects were initiated. This year, water the seeds that were planted the previous year and let things grow. Do not force issues. The 2 personal year certainly favors cooperation and compromise, but marriage entered into in this year is usually because you do not want to be alone. You could find yourself going along with anything and in a controlling situation.

3—This is a party time, a fun time. You may be getting lots of invitations. It's the time to make new friends, express yourself artistically, shop, play, and laugh. Since this is a social year, relationships entered into at this time will be *fun* friendships. Marriage during this year will be *happy* times. But, you may think it will always be *easy going,* and unprepared for the inevitable rough times. A 3 personal day is the best time for a party. Shopping is also favored for this day but you may find yourself buying unnecessary items only because you like the color. (3 is the number of clothes and colors.)

4—This is the time to be a workaholic. Work, stay on schedule, stick to routine, get organized, be practical, and get chores done. Build a structure and foundation for the future. Businesses are often started in this year; but, do not expect profits until your 8 personal year. Marriage in this year usually involves taking on a lot of responsibility, such as caring for someone else's children or being the main breadwinner. It is also an indication that one is looking for security. The 4 personal day is a good time to go on a job interview or start a diet.

5—Expect the unexpected. You won't know what is coming around the corner. Be adventurous, travel, take chances, welcome a change in your schedule, and try something unusual. Experiences will be very unpredictable and unconventional, especially romances. In a 5 personal year you may find yourself in a wild and tumultuous romance with an emphasis on the *sensual* side. If it lasts into the following year, a 6 personal year, it may become serious. The 5 personal year is not a good time to marry. It is for all the wrong reasons, sex or money, and rarely lasts. However, a 5 personal day is a great time to go out looking for romance. Dress up and look your best. You may *unexpectedly* run into someone you want to impress. The 5 personal day is also good for shopping and getting a hair cut.

6—Duty calls. Time is not your own. Others need you. Help people and listen to their problems. Settle arguments and avoid getting into them. Stay close to home, take care of family, welcome responsibility. A 6 personal year is the best time to marry because it is for love. Marriages entered into in this year have a better chance of surviving. Many people move or redecorate in this year because the focus is on the home. The 6 personal day is a good time to clean house; but, avoid travel on this day (unless it is to visit family).

7—This is an introspective period. Rest, recuperate, recharge your battery. You may find yourself sleeping more or staring at the television, because your energy is in your head. Think, plan, wait, reevaluate. Do not force issues. Let things come to you. This is also a spiritual time, not a material time. Money may be slow but it is a good time for investing. This is not the best time to marry. Marriage in this year may mean you need someone to talk to and play psychiatrist to you; or, you may want someone to take care of you. 7 is also the number of secrets. Sometimes people find themselves in a clandestine relationship in this year. Or, you may attract someone who is already married, seeing someone else, or unable to make a commitment because of a restriction or responsibility such as caring for another.

8—This is a material time. Initiate all the things you thought about last year, and actualize all the plans you made. Money, business, finance, and power characterize this time. If that clandestine relationship is still on the scene, this year could clear the way. Marriage in this year usually means money and status are part of the deal. 8 is also the number of fertility. Many women get pregnant in an 8 personal year. If you started a business in your 4 personal year, it could prosper in this year. An 8 personal day is a good time for a workout.

9—This is the time to finish, complete, end, wrap up, and let go of what is no longer needed in your life. You may find you are outgrowing friends, a job, a marriage, or hobbies or interests. Get rid of whatever is no longer working in your life. It is also a spiritual time. Be a humanitarian and do good deeds. Broaden your horizons and attend cultural events. Since this is the ending of a cycle, marriage is unfavorable in the 9 personal year. It is unlikely to last. Although it is good for romance with all the trimmings such as candle light and music. A 9 personal day is a good day for breaking up with someone, but *not* good for a first date. It is also a great day for giving a stage performance, a lecture, or cleaning out your closets.

There are two exceptions to the rule of reducing everything to a single digit. If the numbers add up to an 11 or 22, do *not* reduce to a single digit. Instead write them as a fraction: $11/2$ and $22/4$. These are master numbers and their energy is very powerful. The interpretations are as follows.

$11/2$—This is a highly spiritual and intuitive time. Experiences are non-material. Work in groups. Inspire others by sharing your insights and ideas. Do not strive for personal or material gain. Marriage in the $11/2$ is usually because of shared ideals and dreams.

$22/4$—This is a time to combine the power of both the spiritual and material worlds. Institute large projects and make grand plans. Work to make big dreams big realities. Marriage in the $22/4$ year is usually because of a mutual interest in the inauguration of major projects that reshape the world. A $22/4$ day also is a great day for accomplishment.

I'm giving these meanings to you in a nutshell. For more in-depth meanings, check out any book on basic numerology. My favorite is Florence Campbell's *Your Days Are Numbered*.

When applied to Tarot card reading, knowing the querent's personal vibrations can be very effective for accurate prediction of events. If the cards tell of a new love interest coming onto the scene, calculate the querent's nearest 5 personal month and/or day. If you see in the cards that the breakup of a relationship is imminent, look for the querent's next 9 personal day.

Another technique is to compare the querent's personal year with the cards that appear in the spread. If there are lots of Pentacles, but the querent is in a 7 personal year, it could mean that money is available, but being invested instead. Aces in the spread of someone who is in a *1* personal year reinforce the theme of initiating a new project. These are just some of the countless possible interpretations. By observing your own particular personal vibrations, you can see up close and personal how these influences operate, and learn more about how to incorporate this into your readings.

How exactly do Tarot cards work? The most widely accepted theory is that of psychokinesis or telekinesis. Parapsychologists define this as the ability of the mind to influence the movement of objects. In other words, by concentrating on an inanimate object, someone can actually make that object move. There have been many documented cases of this and its existence is accepted by the parapsychology community, even though it is not fully understood.

Now let's apply this theory of psychokinesis to Tarot cards. If one can mentally affect the movement of objects, isn't it conceivable that one could just as easily *unconsciously* affect the movement or arrangement of Tarot cards? Thus when the querent shuffles the cards and they are laid out in a spread by the reader, they seem to correspond directly with the issues that are on the querent's mind.

"An extraphysical power (now studied in our universities as 'psychokinetic effect')," writes Eden Gray in her book *A Complete Guide to the Tarot*, "affects the unconscious movements of the person shuffling, cutting and laying out the cards, and when they are dealt they seem to fall into positions that inevitably relate to the subject of the reading."

Lynn M. Buess, in his book *The Tarot and Transformation*, elaborates further on this psi theory: "It is written that in conjunction and coincident with the physical body there exists an etheric double—an exact psychic duplication of the physical anatomy. . . . By directed effort of the will, the etheric body can be guided to points far distant from the physical body; this procedure is often referred to as astral projection. It is known that the etheric functions are primarily unconscious. . . . Presumably during a Tarot reading the etheric senses stir the vibrational fields from the individual's subconscious, providing impetus to the selection of the card or cards wherein the symbolism inherently possesses the frequency of vibration corresponding to the querent's life."

There is, however, another theory that may be relevant, and that is Carl Jung's *theory of synchronicity*. Carl Jung developed this theory to apply to the *I Ching*, or *Book of Changes*, but it can easily be applied to the shuffling of Tarot cards.

According to Jung, "whatever happens in a given moment possesses inevitably the quality peculiar to that moment . . . whereas synchronicity takes the coincidence of events in space and time as meaning something more than mere chance namely, a peculiar interdependence of objective events among themselves as well as with the subjective (psychic) states of the observer or observers."

Therefore the psychic or *emotional* state of the querent corresponds with the particular characteristic of that moment of time, when the cards are shuffled. This determines the manner in which they will fall; which is *coincidentally* not random.

Perhaps psychokinesis and/or synchronicity are correct explanations for the workings of Tarot cards. Certainly the common denominator is the psychic or *emotional* state of the querent and this factors into the connection made to the astral level or fourth dimension. Richard Cavendish, in his book *The*

Black Arts, says, "The astral plane, in modern theory, is the one in which desires, emotions and feelings move."

However, with all due respect to these theories, I see the workings of the Tarot differently. I am not going to say that the querent does *not* unconsciously affect the way the cards fall; maybe that really does happen. And maybe it really does happen in conjunction with synchronicity. But I believe something else is going on and that more of the process rests with the reader, not necessarily with the cards that fall in that spread.

I see Tarot cards as a focusing tool that keeps the mind from wandering. When the attention is fixed and the reader is concentrating, psychic energy flows.

As the reader focuses on the cards, the symbols begin to stimulate her subconscious mind. Since the subconscious *naturally* thinks and dreams in symbols, this is very comfortable and there is a shift from the left side of the brain, which is the reasoning area, to the right side, which is the artistic and intuitive area. At this point, insights are mostly coming from the intuitive level. However, at some point, there is transcendence into the purely psychic area. And here is where I see much of the action coming from the reader. This is what I think happens.

Assuming the reader is very focused and centered and the querent is relaxed, at some point the reader will *let go* of the focus on the symbols and literally begin *reading* the querent. She begins to *draw* from the querent. *Drawing* is an old occult technique that most likely came from the East. For certain, the older generation of psychics practiced this technique—maybe even without realizing it. That generation of psychics had skills that were highly impressive. Personally, I don't know if this new crop that is coming up even knows what *drawing* is.

To expound, the reader *draws etheric fluid* from the querent.

Etheric fluid is explained by referring again to the astral level (sometimes called the fourth dimension), which is a less dense level of matter. The etheric level is also a less dense level of matter, but it is nearer to the physical level than the astral level. Just as we have a physical body, we have an etheric body (as already mentioned) and an astral body. This is often re-ferred to as the aura. This etheric body contains a substance known as etheric fluid. By *drawing* on this, a psychic reads the etheric fluid, or literally reads the subconscious mind of the querent.

It is said by metaphysicians and even psychologists that we already know our futures in our deep subconscious minds be-cause unconsciously (or consciously) we are creating them and setting things up for ourselves. What the psychic reader (or Tarot reader, because Tarot is a psychic medium) does is to *draw* this information out (using the occult technique) and bring it to the awareness of the querent during the reading. Many quer-ents report that during a reading they feel pleasantly sleepy or drowsy. This is one of the curious side effects of an intense psy-chic reading. After the reading, when the *drawing* has stopped, the querent feels alert again.

While various cards in the spread may be guideposts for the reader and rouse her intuition, I believe their primary purpose is to serve as an intermediary between the reader and the quer-ent, whereas, the psychic connection made by the reader to the querent is accomplished by the occult technique of *drawing*. Thus there is somewhat of a rotating exchange of energies bouncing from the reader to the cards to the querent and back again. (Since psychic energy and how it works are not under-stood, it is impossible to be certain what exactly is going on.)

However, to me, this is the best explanation for how Tarot cards really work.

The technique of drawing can also be used when reading a crystal ball or tea leaves, or by focusing directly on the querent.

Regarding *drawing of etheric fluid;* many years ago I read about it in an old book, the title of which I have now forgotten. I also remember discussing it in *psychic* circles (in England and the United States) using this exact term. However my recent research yields references to *etheric fluid* only, and nothing in the context of *drawing etheric fluid.* It has been suggested to me that because we have no proper language in which to discuss psychic matters or the mystical experience, this could be causing the confusion. Hence it may be recognized by some people using a different term or different description. This is one of the many frequent frustrations encountered when discussing psychic matters. Therefore I do not know where to refer you for more information on this interesting and rarely mentioned occult technique.

By the way, the technique can be naturally learned by conscious concentration on the cards; that is, by *looking at the cards.* This focus stills the mind and facilitates the quick development of your *intuitive/psychic faculties.* In no time you will become aware of, or *sense,* the subtle interaction between you and the querent.

What does it mean if a card falls out of the deck when the querent is shuffling? There are some readers who think that if a card or cards fall out of the deck during the shuffle, this may be the result of psychokinetic activity as previously explained. There is also the occult maxim that *nothing ever happens by acci-*

dent. In other words, there is a reason for everything. So perhaps this seeming mishap, which may originate in the subconscious mind of the querent, has informative significance and should be immediately interpreted.

I, however, do not make this distinction. I simply pick the fallen card or cards up and ask the querent to reshuffle. I like things to be simple. Adding too many nuances complicates matters and the important points are missed. This is my personal style, and remember it works. You will have to try for yourself to see how you feel about this issue.

What is the difference between astrology, numerology, palmistry, and the Tarot? They are all esoteric disciplines that can give us insight into ourselves and our relationship to the universe. However they are different because they work in different ways, and utilize different data. Astrology uses the birth date, birth place, and exact time of birth. Numerology uses the full name at birth and the birth date. Palmistry uses both hands. And, for a Tarot reading, all that is needed is a deck of Tarot cards, the symbols being the only data used as input.

However there is one very significant difference that places astrology, numerology, and palmistry into one category and leaves the Tarot in another. Astrology, numerology, and palmistry are both *sciences* and *arts*. Astrology and numerology require exact mathematical calculations, and there are rules to scientifically read palms. But all of this must be interpreted and hence these sciences then become arts.

"Astrology is both a science and an art," writes Myrna Lofthus in *A Spiritual Approach to Astrology*. "It is a science, because the setting up of a chart is an exacting process for each factor has to be calculated. As an art, it depends on the astrologer's skill in interpreting the chart." Of palmistry, Marten Steinbach says in his book, *Medical Palmistry*, ". . . modern palmistry is predicated upon a set of criteria as rigid as any in physics." He goes on to say ". . . in reading hands the palmist makes value judgments based in part upon subjective reactions."

Now with the Tarot, there are no exact scientific calculations to interpret, no exact laws to follow, and no scientific methods or formulas to use. There are some helpful guidelines but they have no proven scientific basis. Therefore when reading Tarot cards, information is obtained empirically and one must rely exclusively on one's *intuitive/psychic faculties*. It is this total use of intuition and psychic ability that distinguishes the Tarot from astrology, numerology, and palmistry, and places it in the same category as that of a crystal ball, tea leaves, or rune stones. Whereas the former have a scientific foundation on which to base interpretation and do require the use of *some* intuition, the latter can be described as purely *intuitive/psychic* mediums which serve as focusing tools to keep the mind from wandering.

What do you mean by *intuitive/psychic faculties?* This is a term I made up based on my own personal experience with the Tarot. It is an *intuitive/psychic* medium and aids in the development of our natural *intuitive/psychic faculties*. When reading Tarot cards, you are simultaneously using your intuition and psychic ability.

This term may sound like an oxymoron because intuition and psychic perception could be defined as being very distinct from each other, almost contradictory. But I think there may be a fine line between the two. In a sense, they are both two different ways of receiving information but the actual experience could be described as similar. Rather than debate it, I encourage you to observe for yourself when working with Tarot cards. Meanwhile I shall define intuition and psychic perception (in relation to the Tarot experience) and hopefully give you more of an understanding of what to expect as the development unfolds. Bear with me; these are highly abstract concepts and not easily verbalized; nor are there even enough words in our vocabulary to accurately describe the *otherworldly* experience. As I have said before, language is a big problem!

Intuition, according to *Webster's New World Dictionary*, is "the immediate knowing or learning of something without the *conscious* use of reasoning." Notice, the definition says, "without the *conscious* use of reasoning." It does not say that reasoning is not used. It says one is not aware of the reasoning process.

Marten Steinbach in his book, *Medical Palmistry*, elaborates: "Intuition may be defined as the instantaneous synthesis below the level of consciousness of observed details leading to the formation of judgments, only the results rising into consciousness."

What both of these definitions are describing is a flash of insight that everyone has had at one time or another, a sudden realization that seems to come out of nowhere. It may seem illogical and unexplainable but you know it is accurate. This is intuition; and, on some level, even if you have not been aware of it, you *have* used your reasoning ability. You have made what Marten Steinbach calls "the intuitive leap . . . to the extrapolated conclusion."

Relating the *intuitive leap* to Tarot card reading, the symbols are actually providing the basis for reasoning (on an intuitive, but unconscious, level). When looking at the symbols, you make a connection with them (on an intuitive, but unconscious level). This connection gives you flashes of insight which allow you to make the *intuitive leap*.

While intuition is considered to be a function of the intellect (unconscious *reasoning* is involved), psychic perception occurs on the emotional level. (Remember emotions are in the astral realm.) With intuition, we *know*. With psychic perception, we *feel* or sense something (the *sixth sense*). We perceive something which goes, according to *Webster's*, "beyond natural or known physical processes." With psychic perception, it's as if something passes through us or we see it in our mind's eye (clairvoyance); and, we know it through our *sixth sense*. It is a much more subtle awareness than the intuitive flash. When psychic channels are triggered, the impressions received seem to transcend or bear no relation at all to the symbols.

Eden Gray, in her book *A Complete Guide to the Tarot*, says "Perhaps you are psychic; the cards then will really come alive for you. . . . Those who do not feel that they are psychic will soon find, however, that they are developing a sixth sense. . . ."

What can I do to further develop my *intuitive/psychic faculties?* I have repeatedly emphasized the importance of a calm mind and the standard technique to accomplish this is meditation. Not meditation on Tarot cards (although I do not discourage it); but old-fashioned, traditional, eastern meditation—the way the yogis do it. Meditation promotes relaxation. It is centering and helps you to focus and concentrate. When you are relaxed, psychic energy naturally and easily flows.

There are many meditation classes available offering a variety of techniques, all of which are beneficial. If you combine meditation with yoga exercises and breathing exercises, the results will be even better.

Be warned, however; do not go into a meditation or yoga class announcing your intentions to develop psychic ability. This is frowned upon by yoga masters. Indeed, yoga does develop many extraordinary powers, such as psychic ability and the ability to levitate. These supernormal powers, called *siddhis*, begin appearing after years and years of discipline and practice. The traditional yogi is very spiritual and considers these siddhis to be distracting and tries to ignore them. According to traditional eastern belief, the yogi's only objective is to reach enlightenment, and the display of paranormal powers is egocentric and not consistent with spiritual goals.

Another technique I recommend is *Silva Mind Control*. I was introduced to this many years ago and have used it in conjunction with traditional meditation. *Silva Mind Control*, also known as the *Silva Method*, is a scientifically based program that teaches how, through controlled relaxation, it is possible to tap into the unlimited potentials of the mind.

By using a simple technique, alpha waves can quickly be produced. These are brain waves that allow the mind to function at deeper, more effective levels. When the mind is at alpha level, one is relaxed and can easily solve problems, think creatively, and develop intuition and psychic ability. Other benefits include improved learning and memory skills, maintaining a positive mental attitude, and eliminating bad habits.

Silva Mind Control is really a *speedy* form of meditation and the concentration techniques are similar to those taught in the East by yogis and Zen masters; but the *Silva Method* is more attuned to the western mentality and lifestyle.

Most meditation instructors recommend thirty minutes two times a day. There are even Tarot instructions to meditate on one card for thirty minutes. However, in an era that coined the term 24/7, when was the last time you found thirty minutes for lunch? In this busy and tumultuous age, when time is so precious, the benefits of any kind of meditation become more significant than ever. While it would be nice to be able to sit for long periods every day, for most people it is virtually an impossibility. This should not be discouraging. Even sitting alone for only a few minutes each day, finding your center and reflecting on the *here and now* will yield positive results.

Will following a special diet enhance my *intuitive/psychic faculties?* My answer to this question will probably surprise you. But I am speaking from experience, and, in my experience: No! Following a special diet will not enhance your *intuitive/psychic* abilities.

I have been on junk food binges for days, ingesting hamburgers, French fries, candy, and caffeine and noticed no diminishment at all in my ability to read with clarity.

Nor have I noticed an increase in my intuition when following a healthy diet; although I certainly felt a lot better. I have experimented with macrobiotics, vegetarianism, and a *food combining* program and found no enhancement or decrease in my *intuitive/psychic faculties*. I do maintain, however, that because psychic work can be so draining, it is important to keep your stamina up, and the way to do that is to eat well.

However, there is one practice that *temporarily* enhanced my faculties. Many years ago I was living on Long Island, New York, and reading at psychic fairs, discos, and restaurants. Of course, the disco and restaurant work was done in the evening, so I would skip dinner and spend about three to four hours reading on an empty, growling stomach. I did, however, drink lots of fluids: water and diet sodas. My readings were incredible! They were so sharp I literally pulled insights out of the air.

The thinking is that it takes energy to digest food and if your stomach is full, the digestive system is, of course, using energy to digest the food. But if the stomach is empty, there is more energy available to be directed towards psychic channels.

However, there is a serious downside to this practice. After the stint, I'd be so hungry from the low blood sugar, I'd rush to an inviting Long Island Greek diner and *pig out* (literally gorge myself) on cheese omelets, toasted buttered bagels, hash browns, and lemon meringue pie. Years later a nutritionist told me it was very unhealthy to throw the blood sugar off, and, of course, this was not helpful in my chronic *battle of the bulge*. So please don't try this unless your body is strong and healthy enough to withstand the stress.

There is also a theory, according to occultists, that the slightly *starved* body, that is an extremely thin person, has an advantage because the etheric body is already slightly loosened, making that individual naturally more psychic. In the answer to the question, *How exactly do Tarot cards work?* there is mention of the unconscious projection of the etheric body. Therefore being really skinny may give easier access to the fourth dimension. Not very encouraging for an overweight society; and, from my experience, not at all a necessity. This is just more added information you can try incorporating if you are strong-willed enough to make it past Ben & Jerry's!

While still on the subject of diet; Dion Fortune in *Psychic Self Defence*, gives her two cents by criticizing the Theosophical Society's insistence that vegetarianism is an absolute necessity for occult training. Dion Fortune and I both agree that a vegetarian diet is not for everyone and, unless thoroughly understood, can cause severe problems after a considerable period of time. We also both agree that a healthy, well-balanced diet of moderate portions of food is the most sustaining for spirituality.

How can I *already* know my future? Isn't it interesting how one question leads to another and one answer overlaps into another? When expounding on Tarot cards, there is a thin line between the technical and the philosophical.

I have mentioned that metaphysicians and psychologists say we already know our futures because we are unconsciously (or consciously) setting things up for ourselves. It is also agreed by metaphysicians, theologians, and psychologists that our thoughts have power. We are the sum total of our thoughts. Literally, as we think, so we are. To reiterate: thoughts (emotions, feelings) exist on the astral level. So when we think something, the thought is a reality on the astral level. A powerful thought, charged with strong emotion, will then work its way down to the physical level, where it becomes a tangible reality in our lives. This is why we are told to *think happy thoughts!*

This is better explained by the myth about an Egyptian god, Thoth; also, known in Greek circles as Hermes Trismegistus. I remember one source describing him as half-man and half-god; his father being the god Hermes and his mother a mere mortal woman. Regardless of his ancestry, legend has it that he gave to the world an inscribed emerald tablet containing a valuable occult axiom. It boils down to these famous words: *as above, so below.*

This simple formula describes the fundamental law of the

cosmos, summing up the nature of the universe. It can be interpreted on different levels. In plain terms, there is an order to
the entire universe. Notice how the structure of the atom bears
a very similar resemblance to the solar system. *As above, so below*. This is also the metaphysical rationale for the validity of
astrology. As the planets move about in the sky, the *symbolic interpretations* of their movements correspond with events that
take place on earth. *As above, so below.*

As I have said, this *universal truth* even plays out in the astral
world, according to cosmic law and order. The astral world is
totally governed by thought. Our thoughts, conscious or unconscious, take hold on the astral level, which ultimately becomes reflected on the earthly level. *As above, so below.*

Richard Wilhelm, in his introduction to the *I Ching*, writes,
". . . every event in the visible world is the effect of an 'image',
that is, of an idea in the unseen world [the astral level]. Accordingly, everything that happens on earth is only a reproduction, as it were, of an event in a world beyond our sense
perception; as regards its occurrence in time, it is later than the
suprasensible event." In other words, when you think something; it takes place on the astral level; and, then at a later
time, it happens/manifests here on earth.

Listen up! Wilhelm goes on to say, "The holy men and sages,
who are in contact with those higher spheres [psychics who can
connect with the fourth dimension], have access to these ideas
through direct intuition and, are therefore able to intervene de-
cisively in the events of the world." Therefore since an event
has already taken place in the fourth dimension, the psychic is
seeing that event in the fourth dimension and foreseeing it as a
future event that will happen in the life of the querent. The

psychic is telling the querent something the querent has already set up for herself (on the astral level) by thinking it!

I know I am repeating myself, here, but it is unavoidable. Working with the Tarot allows for the development of the intuition. As the intuition develops, contact with higher realms is made, along with an attuning to your higher consciousness. This means you have an increased awareness of the fourth dimension or the astral level, where your thoughts take place and initially become realities. As awareness of your higher consciousness increases, you begin to realize you are responsible for everything you are bringing into your life. In other words, you are creating your own future. Call it enlightenment or good old-fashioned maturity; but, for certain, it is a change in consciousness.

I vividly remember when first starting the study of the Tarot along with other forms of divination, I was told all of this by older and wiser people. I was clearly advised *future-telling* was not what it was all about and that there was a deeper, more spiritual significance to be gained by esoteric inquiries (and that was self-awareness). But I refused to listen. Surely to read the future was to have power! Eventually, after several years of growth, I came to realize that what *the elders* had told me really was true; the power was *within* me. *As above, so below.*

You will also notice after reading Tarot cards for diverse types of people, that it is more difficult to predict the future for those who already have a degree of cosmic consciousness. People with awareness are in control of their lives (and their futures) and take responsibility for the choices they make. Nor would these types be thrown off their feet by external, uncontrollable events. Their inner fortitude, as acquired by this cosmic consciousness or mature approach to life, would sustain them through difficult times.

Another revelation coinciding with spiritual development is that you realize there is virtually nothing supernatural about *fortune-telling*. It is a perfectly natural pursuit because it is in accordance with natural cosmic law.

A closing thought: The Magician, the first card in the deck, is in my opinion the depiction of this classic metaphysical maxim. His right hand is raised toward the heavens (*as above*) as he draws power down and passes it through his left hand, which points to the earth (*so below*). He lives in harmony with cosmic law by balancing the elements (earth, water, air, and fire) as represented by the symbols on the table before him.

If I shuffle the cards again, will I get the same answer? This is something men frequently ask me; they like testing the cards. But remember my previous explanation; it really isn't the cards anyway. While the same cards may very well turn up over and over again, I believe the information is not directly coming from the cards but, instead, from the psychic interaction with the querent. Therefore playing with the cards will cause nothing more than disturbing confusion.

Refer to the *I Ching* or *Book of Changes*. The fourth hexagram, *Youthful Folly*, says: "At the first oracle I inform him. If he asks two or three times, it is importunity. If he importunes, I give no information." In other words, if you play with the oracle, the oracle will play with you.

Only in the beginning, when you are learning to read the cards, should you be testing them. After that period, they should be treated with great respect.

If you are uncomfortable with an answer that the Tarot has given, you can either wait twenty-four hours before asking it again or try using a different spread. A different spread may give you more in-depth information. But *playing* with the cards to test them or because you do not like the answer they have given you is fruitless, unwise, and a virtual exercise in futility.

Plus remember the effect emotions have on the reading. Anxiety and agitation are obstructions. If you have a strong emotional investment in a matter, try meditating for several minutes to calm the mind. A deep meditation is centering and opens the psychic channels.

Can I read Tarot cards for myself? This is a personal matter. I think the issue of an emotional investment is an even stronger obstacle when attempting to read for oneself. Dion Fortune agrees: "It is well known that no seer can skry for himself in any matter in which he himself is intimately concerned."

I find it very difficult to be objective with myself when concerned about a specific situation. My emotions and wishful thinking get in the way of accepting the answer the Tarot cards give me. However, a friend of mine, who is an excellent reader, answers questions for herself all the time and always gets accurate insights.

On the other hand, if I want to see what comes out and I am not looking for anything specific, I tend to get some amazing insights. Unfortunately, at times I can only make sense out of the reading in retrospect by looking back over the notes of which cards came up.

Certainly during the learning phases, you *should* give yourself readings. This is how you learn. But further down the road, this may be another exercise in futility. Again you are going to have to experiment and find what works for you. Note taking for this is invaluable, and remember the benefits of meditating!

How far into the future can you see with the Tarot? There are spreads that can cover a lifetime but personally I find them valueless. People can grow and change, and time for that growth must be allowed. The classic Tarot maxim, *the only thing constant in life is change*, hints at how we can change/control our lives by the choices we make.

To rephrase previously discussed concepts: while there may be some things that are predestined or beyond our control, not everything is written in stone and, according to occultists, we can control our lives. In more instances than we'd like to ad-mit, the future is really determined by the choices we make or how we choose to respond (not react) to the challenges the universe presents to us. Metaphysicians believe we can have free will by making *conscious* choices in life.

The ancient Chinese clearly recognized that the universe is always in a state of flux, and based the *I Ching* on this metaphysical observation. Hence the changing lines in the hexagrams were developed to express various forms of transfor-mations, and to give the inquirer *choices* of how to effectively deal with situations.

Applying this to any form of divination, the inevitable pos-sibility of change and growth must be allowed for before long-term predictions are made. Therefore I am comfortable with an accurate projection of about six months to one year into the fu-ture with Tarot cards.

An extra note: there are some traditionalists who refuse to use esoteric disciplines to foretell the future, preferring to use them as tools for self-awareness only. They firmly believe that, if you tell a querent too much about the future, it becomes a *self-fulfilling* prophecy. The querent will set it up for herself— unconsciously, of course—and make absolutely no effort to initiate the necessary changes in her life for self-improvement.

Meanwhile, I have been talking about future-telling with Tarot cards. But sometimes just the opposite happens. I briefly mentioned this in Chapter 2. At times there is the problem of distinguishing between the past, present, and future. Instead of projecting into the future, you may go backwards into the past and pick up past issues very easily. This is because the effects of a past issue may still have a strong hold on the querent and on the *emotional variables*. Remember, emotions exist on the astral level and the reader is picking up on emotions. I also previously mentioned that when tapping into other dimensions our perceptions of time and space are altered or transcended. The past, present, and future are actually merged into one stream of consciousness. I admit this is really a watered-down explanation in describing the experience on the *shadowy plane*. Again, I defend the inability to clearly do so because language or lack of proper language is really the problem. However, this altered perception is another factor that adds to the complication of time and Tarot cards, and explains why the direction in which the reading goes may *appear* to be uncontrollable (i.e. going backward in time or forward in time). I am pointing this out so when you begin reading for others, you will not be surprised if this happens. It is important to know what kinds of experiences to expect. The fourth dimension is a peculiar realm!

With so many Tarot decks to choose from, which is the best to use? As you can see, I prefer the Rider-Waite Tarot deck. I think it is the easiest to work with, easiest to teach, and easiest to learn. It is a very traditional deck that was developed around the early 1900s. The Rider-Waite Tarot deck is a creation of the combined efforts of Arthur Edward Waite and Pamela Colman Smith. Waite was a brilliant occultist with a deep understanding of the Tarot and its mystical symbolism. Smith was a brilliant and talented artist. Both were members of the very famous Order of The Golden Dawn, a powerful occult organization, which no longer exists. Waite gave Ms. Smith specific instructions for the drawings, and together they developed a beautiful, colorful, and alive deck of cards filled with rich mystical symbolism. This deck has been in print for almost one hundred years, and is considered a classic among Tarot cards.

Several years ago, out of curiosity, I experimented with two other decks. One was designed by Aleister Crowley, the notorious and reputedly nefarious magician, who was also at one time a member of The Golden Dawn. Crowley's deck is laden with heavy dark symbolism, and reflects his allegedly sinister personality. I used this deck for one spread during a private consultation. I then expanded on the reading by switching back to the Rider-Waite deck and saw *death* in the cards, a story I recount in Chapter 6. I took it as an ominous portent, and never used Crowley's deck again!

Around that time I also tried another deck, the Astro-Mythological Cards designed by Marie Lenormand. Mlle. Lenormand was a famous Tarot card reader, counsel to the Emperor Napoleon, his wife, Josephine, and many prominent aristocrats. Her accurate but unwelcome predictions so infuriated Napoleon that, on two occasions, he threw her in prison! Mlle. Lenormand's cards are lovely but they never clicked with me.

I do, however, encourage students to sample other decks, after they have had some experience with the Rider-Waite deck.
There are countless decks currently on the market and more
and more appearing yearly.

How do you feel about Tarot cards for children? *Many moons
ago*, when I began reading professionally, I was adamantly
against Tarot cards for children. I thought it was totally inappropriate. However as I began entertaining at bar mitzvahs, the
Tarot began increasing in popularity, and there were many re-
quests for readings for children by the children themselves.
Alas, one must change with the times! Reluctantly one night I
tried an experiment. Starting with a new deck, I took about
one-third of the cards out of the deck. This included all the *difficult* cards, such as Death, The Tower, and many of the Swords.
(By the way, when I read at parties I use the miniature deck. It
is small and much easier to shuffle quickly.) The results were as-
tounding! It was a great night. The children loved it and the
readings were light and fun. I saw pets, happy days at summer
camp, and vacations to foreign countries. I continue using my
children's deck for young people up to fourteen years of age.

As for your child wanting to learn how to read Tarot cards,
this is of course a personal matter for each parent. I would suggest removing, as I have done, the *heavy* cards. I have also noticed that children are more sensitive to the imagery than
adults; perhaps because they are not yet programmed by rational thinking and still in touch with many of their intuitive
feelings. This is a good thing in a way and could work towards
making them excellent Tarot readers.

I remember one thirteen-year-old boy looking at the 3 of

Swords. "Yuch!" He remarked. "This looks awful!" An honest opinion, out of the mouths of babes.

In another instance, I was reading at a little children's Halloween party. I wore a witch's hat and attempted to play a sort of Go-Fish Tarot with the children, while throwing astro-dice. There really isn't much you can tell tiny tots, and I had suggested to the mother that she call a theatrical school and hire an actor to play a character. It would have been a lot less expensive. But the mother wanted the *real McCoy*. I read for some of the nannies and other mothers and tried to keep the children busy. One little five-year-old girl became enthralled with the cards. She went through them one-by-one and fell in love with the 9 of Cups (a wish granted) and the 6 of Cups (children playing and gift-giving). So intense was her attraction to these particular cards, she wouldn't give them back to me.

"I like these!" she told me with glee. "I'm keeping them for myself."

It was amazing how a little child, who could neither read nor write, could intuitively connect with the beautiful symbolism of these two cards. Fortunately by the end of the party, she lost interest and threw them on the couch, allowing for an easy retrieval.

What I have heard from some parents is that their child quickly becomes disenchanted with the cards because the instructions are too hard to figure out. My instructions should be very easy for a child to follow because my method is in tune with genuine *childlikeness*.

Why are Tarot cards becoming so popular? Fascination with Tarot cards has endured for centuries, but their recent surge in popularity definitely coincides with the New Millennium shift in consciousness, which also accounts for the increased interest in *all* New Age pursuits.

As we started moving towards the new century, many people began experiencing other dimensions and perceiving a higher consciousness. This will become even more pronounced over the next several years. In March 2003 the planet Uranus moved into Pisces where it will remain until March 2011. Uranus is the great awakener and Pisces is the psychic sign, ruling intuition, feelings, telepathy, mysticism, and spirituality. During this time, psychic energy will be abundantly floating around, and psychic skills such as clairvoyance and telepathy will be easier to develop. From April 2011 to the end of January 2026, Neptune will also be rolling around in the sign of Pisces, Neptune's natural ruler. Thus the increased awareness of other realms and the spiritual activities associated with them will be on the rise during that period too. So the next two and a half decades, hopefully, will be marked by great advancement in our spiritual evolution.

This is where Tarot cards come in. They make a perfect fit with the astrological trend of the coming times; and their popularity will become even more widespread as we move forward into what might very well be the Age of Enlightenment.

The Tarot raises spiritual awareness and fosters the development of intuition; and, remember, the cards serve as focusing tools for directing psychic energy! It is my deep conviction that these mysterious cards, laden with ancient esoteric symbols conveying eternal wisdom, will play an integral role in the future development of our spiritual growth. Tarot cards will become universally recognized as invaluable instruments that illuminate the path connecting us to our higher selves.

Check out the eighteenth card, The Moon. It represents the psychic world and all its infinite manifestations.

Is it important to be familiar with the history of the Tarot cards' symbolism? Tarot cards were designed with symbols taken from many different ancient cultures. Perhaps this is why it is so difficult to attribute their origins to one particular civilization.

While the historical background and details of the esoteric meanings of each symbol (as it relates to a particular culture) would be very interesting, I think it defeats the entire purpose of the cards.

"The aim of . . . symbols . . . was to reach man's higher centers [the higher self], to transmit to him ideas inaccessible to the intellect. . . ." This is from P. D. Ouspensky's book *In Search of the Miraculous*. Ouspensky is, of course, quoting George Gurdjieff, a controversial spiritual teacher of the last century.

"Symbolism is the language of the subconscious," says the late renowned Tarot reader Richard Gardner in his book *The Tarot Speaks*. "In the middle ages we communicated far more by symbols than we do now. Shops, for instance, invariably used signs, not written names, so that in those days our minds would have been more practiced in symbology than now." (Centuries ago, most people did not read or write; thus, before reading became widespread, symbols were used in everyday life. A tavern displayed a mug of ale; an optician displayed a pair of glasses; or a shoemaker displayed a shoe or boot.) Richard Gardner goes on to say, "This is a considerable loss to our intuition, which thinks and manifests in symbols. . . ."

"Symbols can be thought of as *psychic transmitters*," writes Alfred Douglas in his book *The Tarot*.

By *studying, thinking,* and *intellectualizing* you are blocking the purpose of the symbols and creating a barrier to the development of the *intuitive/psychic faculties*. Keep in mind that it is the symbols which make that direct connection to the higher self. It is also important to remember that the cards were not originally designed to be a fortune-telling device. Therefore the historical background of the symbols may not even be relevant to the divinatory meanings. This intellectual pursuit would lead to abject confusion. I give it a big *thumbs down!* If your curiosity gets the best of you, I suggest you wait to study the history of the symbols only after having made the intuitive connection with the cards.

Is it true that a Tarot reading cannot be recorded on tape?
From my experience, it is impossible many times to record a psychic reading of any kind. I do qualify this by saying *many times,* but not always. Psychic energy appears to have a tendency to interfere with mechanical equipment. This has been observed by parapsychology researchers during experiments and by psychics when attempting to record a psychic session. The reason why is not known. These energies are very subtle and not scientifically understood. Therefore we cannot predict what they will do. Nevertheless, I have personally been witness to this phenomenon.

This first time was at a séance, and it was with *my* tape recorder! It worked perfectly before the séance. I tested it and retested it, then placed it in the center of the circle. I had been warned by others that it would not record the event, but I didn't believe it. Sure enough, the machine did not pick up the sounds of the séance, except for some barely audible chanting. After the séance, the tape recorder worked perfectly again!

Other incidents during my career include two clients complaining to me that the readings they had recorded did not come out clearly on the tape. All they heard was a muffled blur.

Their tape recorders worked perfectly before the consultations began. The clients tested them. But this is what can happen when an intense psychic level is reached during a session.

Having been informed by other readers of the risks of recording a session, I had advised both of these individuals to take notes instead of record. They both thought that would be too much of a task, and insisted on taping. Of course they were angry with me when it didn't work. Now I *insist* clients take notes or record at their own risk.

Can spells be cast with Tarot cards? By arranging the cards in certain combinations that pictorially suggest the desired situation, it is theoretically possible to cast a spell with Tarot cards. This is to be done in conjunction with other tools such as candles and/or incense, certain incantations, as well as strong intense creative visualization.

But the cards, candles, incense, incantations, and other tools are really nothing more than props used to set the frame of mind of the subconscious. These tools, in themselves, do not increase the effectiveness of the spell. The real key to casting spells is rarely revealed in books.

In answer to the question *How can I already know my future?* I explain how everything manifests in the astral world first and then happens on the physical plane where we live. So in order to effectively cast a spell, regardless of which tools you use, the desired event must take place on the astral level first. And, how is that possible?

Keep in mind that emotions and feelings exist on the astral level. When performing any kind of ritual *magick* the *feeling* that accompanies the desired situation must be a part of the ritual. For instance, if you are casting a spell to win $50,000,000 in the lottery, you must *feel* as if you have already won that $50,000,000. You must *feel* as if it has already happened. Try this exercise. Pause for a few seconds. Then ask yourself how you would *feel* if you had just found out you had won the lottery. What would you be thinking? You probably had a great feeling of soaring joy. Then you started thinking of all the things you'd do with the money. This is the key to effective creative visualization and making spells work. The emotion must be there. You must maintain that emotion constantly. Then it will take root on the astral level, and eventually on the physical/earth plane.

Try another example. How would you *feel* if Mr. *Right* said he was in love with you and asked you to marry him. You'd probably have a wonderful warm feeling. It is that *feeling* that must accompany a love spell in order for it to work. You must feel as if you are being loved by Mr. *Right*. This is a great occult secret! It is the emotion that sets things into motion. But performing spells always comes with a price that is usually unexpected, because you can inadvertently be unleashing energies that lead to unforeseen consequences and unanticipated side-effects. *Be careful what you wish for, you just might get it.* This is one of the down sides you must be aware of.

The other drawback is that you can never control when the spell will actually take effect or happen. As I have already explained, let *George* take care of the timing. Whenever it happens, it happens. I personally have never tried to cast a spell with Tarot cards, but I know of three experiences from other people. Based on what they told me, if it works, there is a price to be paid.

Elizabeth was an English gal I met while living in Spain. After a violent incident, she confided in me how she had cast a love spell on her Spanish boyfriend, Francisco. (By the way, love spells are the most commonly done and the most risky. This is an excellent example of how uncertain the outcome can be.) Elizabeth had been living in Spain when she met Francisco. They went together for awhile; then, he broke up with her. Sad and despondent, she returned to England, still in love with him.

She decided to turn to magick, and arranged three Tarot cards in a certain order. The Lovers in the middle to indicate the desired situation. The Knight of Pentacles on one side, to represent Francisco. And the Queen of Cups on the other side to symbolize herself. Along with that she had a special love ring designed. The setting was made of copper, the stone was green. Green is the color of Venus, the planet of love. The ring was made during a favorable time of the planet Venus, when love aspects were harmonious. Constantly wearing the magickal ring, she meditated on the Tarot card arrangement for several months.

Then Francisco came to England to get her. Together they returned to Spain and took up residence in a rooming house. Everything was fine for a year and a half. Then Elizabeth accidentally got pregnant. She wanted to go to England to have an abortion. But Francisco, being a native of a strict Catholic country, had strong objections to abortion. He was also an alcoholic. One night in a drunken rage, he beat Elizabeth beyond recognition. She came running over to my apartment and stayed for a few days. Then she went back to Francisco, who beat her up again. Finally I managed to get her on a plane back to England, where she took care of the matter.

Right before she got on the plane, she gave me the love ring suggesting it might help with the problems I was having with my Spanish boyfriend. But having observed her predicament, I was too terrified to wear it.

This is a classic example of a spell that worked like a charm, but with an added unimaginable twist. It was definitely *not happily ever after*.

Another woman recounted to me how she cast a Tarot spell on a man she had yearned to meet. Jane had a crush on an up-and-coming actor. She used a grouping of four Tarot cards: The Lovers, The Star (to symbolize his *rising* star), the 3 of Cups (to symbolize meeting in a social situation), and the 9 of Pentacles to represent herself. In the middle, she placed his photograph.

Together with that, she did a candle burning ritual: a green candle for love, a pink candle for passion, and a red candle for *lovemaking*. She spent an intense week putting energy into casting this spell.

Seven months passed and nothing happened. Remember, things happen on their own time. All of sudden a door opened. She met someone who agreed to make the introduction. This offer was also accompanied by reliable information that her *dream lover* had a serious drug problem. Suddenly she saw him as a dreadful *nightmare*. This was not what she had expected. Wisely, she declined the invitation. But for months thereafter she was consumed with anger. She had invested energy and time into this, only to be miserably disappointed. She vowed never to cast another spell again.

These stories have been about love spells—without a doubt, the most hazardous. The next story is about job security. Even a spell like that comes with a price.

I met Betsy many years ago through out mutual interest in Tarot cards. She knew a lot about them, and one night we stayed up late giving each other readings and exchanging information.

Betsy had an excellent job in a public relations firm. She had a large office, a good salary, and a substantial chunk of power. After five years with the company, things began to sour. There was talk of a total reorganization and her job was on the line.

She thought a Tarot spell would easily remedy the problem. She selected several cards to portray the situation she wanted to maintain. The Magician to represent the power she had; the 10 of Pentacles to represent the company and its continued prosperity; the Queen of Pentacles for her significator; and she threw in the 4 of Pentacles, the Ace of Pentacles, and the Ace of Wands to complete the story. An ardent practitioner of positive thinking and creative visualization, she meditated on this configuration every night and visualized herself sitting in her office with the *feeling* that everything was all right. And so it was for one year.

Then everything exploded. Her company merged with a larger firm and a house-cleaning began. The inevitable was unpreventable and more brutal than could possibly ever have been imagined. Betsy was forced to find another job. She told me she learned a valuable lesson from this. There are some things in life you cannot control and at times it is better to let go of your desire and trust in the judgment of the *infinite intelligence*.

Why do fortune-tellers wear shawls? A frivolous question I am occasionally asked, usually by men. However, I have a serious answer.

Obviously this style was taken from the Gypsies, who were the first real Tarot *fortune-tellers*. But I have another theory that deserves some consideration. Many psychics, including myself, frequently feel chilled or quite cold when giving readings, and trance mediums have noticed that there is a chill in the air when spirits are present. Even parapsychologists have observed and documented this. When testing mediums and a *manifestation* (or spirit presence) is about to take place, there is an extremely noticeable drop in temperature that can also be measured. Although this is not scientifically understood, nor even a proven fact, it is a consistent observation. Furthermore, according to occultists, *all* astral world phenomena appear to be accompanied by lowered temperatures. Since reading Tarot cards does involve generating psychic energy, this could be a hypothesis which accounts for the *big chill* and the necessity of a warm shawl.

Is it really bad luck to buy a Tarot deck for yourself and must you wait for someone to give it to you as a gift? I have heard this too, and I think it is nothing more than a silly superstition. I have no idea where it came from. My belief is that if you are drawn to Tarot cards, you should be enjoying them, regardless of whether you purchase them yourself or receive them as a gift.

I did *not* receive my cards as a gift. I was fascinated by them and bought my first deck in 1967. Perhaps I was *guided* to do so. Whatever, I can truthfully say this has never brought me any bad luck; instead, the exact opposite! Tarot cards have added fulfillment and joy to my life. In all my years, I met only one woman who told me she had received the cards as a gift. She confessed to having no interest in them whatsoever, and they remained unused, stored in an attic.

Why do some people say Tarot cards are evil and the devil's work? Prohibition against playing cards (including Tarrochi) became common in many parts of Europe almost as soon as the cards appeared on the scene (around the mid-fourteenth century). The cards themselves were not deemed bad but they were used by many people for *gambling*, and *that* was thought to be immoral or the *devil's work*! Ironically it was the Church that initially banned the cards, not the Grand Inquisitors.

When the Inquisitions began around the thirteenth century, about one hundred years prior to the appearance of the cards, occultism of any kind was branded as evil and heretical. However, Tarot cards were not lumped into the occult category until people started using them for *fortune-telling*. (This was most likely started by the Gypsies upon their arrival in Europe around the end of the fourteenth century or early fifteenth century.) The Catholic Church at one time banned Tarot cards, but now no longer forbids them.

Nevertheless many religious fundamentalists, especially in specific geographical localities, still hold to this antiquated thinking and vehemently condemn Tarot cards, astrology, and the occult claiming these esoteric pursuits are the *work of the devil*. These fundamentalists can be quite fanatical and aggressive. While reading Tarot cards at a small college in Kentucky, two students stood over me praying, insisting I had devils in me. (You *can't* make this stuff up!) Another college in the South received complaints by a few students about my appearance on the campus, because it was threatening to their religious beliefs. I went on with the show, even though the turnout was small; and, fortunately, there was no heckling nor disruption.

I have also been personally challenged with questions specifically about The Devil, the fifteenth card in the deck, because of the inverted pentagram. This is said to be the sign of the devil. ". . . a reversed pentagram, with two points upwards, is a symbol of the Devil and attracts sinister forces because it is upside down . . ." writes Richard Cavendish in his book, *The Black Arts*. Although, *I* view this as an innocuous symbol that has no more power than one chooses to give to it, religious opponents of the occult have suggested to me that it really *does* have malevolent power. This small minority of ultra-right-wing fundamentalists and evangelical Christians actually believe the devil is a real external force, tempting everyone to do wrong. Therefore, according to these fundamentalists, it is the inverted pentagram *precisely* that makes Tarot cards evil because it is evidence that the devil, himself, comes with the cards!

I was stunned by the idea. It's ludicrous. How can anyone seriously believe in this modern age of science that a deck of cards made of paper and ink are bad because of a symbol?

The devil is traditionally defined as an abstract concept. Richard Cavendish writes in *The Black Arts*, "The Devil is a legacy of the widespread human tendency to attribute the origin of evil to non-human influences." The thinking in our current times is that putting blame on the devil is a convenient excuse for avoiding personal responsibility for one's actions. Yet, there are those who still strongly hold to what I call the *Inquisition mentality*.

Flip Wilson, a brilliant comedian who is no longer with us, created a hilarious character, Geraldine. A zany woman, she blamed the devil for everything she did wrong.

"The devil made me do it!" Flip Wilson would say in a high-pitched voice. The audience would roar with laughter.

I have always looked at the card of The Devil as the opposite of The Lovers, the sixth card. To me, The Lovers suggests innocence. But The Devil suggests greed, jealousy, pride, and en-slavement to materialism; negatives indeed, but not Lucifer, himself.

Eden Gray writes of this controversial card in *A Complete Guide to the Tarot*, "There is no Devil except of man's own cre-ation, and here it is evident that men are chained by their own wrong choices." One can choose to take the *high road* or the *low road.*

Returning to the Inquisitions, as soon as they started, occult secrets began disappearing. Perhaps their keepers decided to take them to their graves out of fear or tightened up the oral tradition deliberately to make these secrets less available. This may be what has caused our spiritual evolution to lag so far be-hind our material evolution. Now, more than a thousand years since the first Inquisitions were held, many people are disillu-sioned with institutionalized religion and looking to New Age studies for spiritual fulfillment. Thus, despite the critics' con-demnation, the occult is no longer underground.

Do you have to be psychic to read Tarot cards? Let's clarify one thing first. We are all born with psychic ability. As people grow up many tend to suppress these psychic powers because we are taught to trust only our reason and to accept only informa-tion that is perceived through our five senses.

Tarot cards help us to get back in touch with our inherent psychic ability. Most people will definitely notice an increase in their *intuitive/psychic* abilities after working with the Tarot for only a very short time. Granted some will be more adept then others; but, nevertheless everyone has the ability to a de-gree.

Can you pick stocks with Tarot cards? Someone called me from Chicago asking me to do this. At that time the stock market was so volatile I would have told everyone who asked me that question *not* to even invest in stocks, no matter how they were selected! (Even at the time of writing this book, the volatility of the stock market must be causing investors severe heartburn.)

However regardless of the volatility, even when there is a strong bull market I would advise against the use of Tarot cards for picking stocks or any investment, for that matter. This is because of the emotional sensitivity of Tarot cards. If one is anxious about an investment (and who isn't?) this can affect the reading, making the interpretation unclear.

I was once asked to give a reading about the *performance* of a particular stock. It wasn't doing well and a gentleman wanted to know if he should sell it. I asked him to pick three cards. He pulled the Wheel of Fortune, The Tower, and 5 of Pentacles. It didn't make sense. I asked him to pick another three cards for clarification. He pulled The Sun, 3 of Swords, and 5 of Cups. I suggested the stock might suddenly go up, but there would be quick profit taking and then it would suddenly go down again. I further suggested it would be a good idea to keep a close eye on it and perhaps to put a *stop limit* on it. That means when a stock reaches a certain price, going up or down, it is activated and later automatically executed (sold) at that price or even better. This gives the investor *down side* protection. Two weeks later the investor called to tell me that all of a sudden the stock began to rise. When it reached the price at which he had bought it, he sold immediately. Apparently other investors had the same strategy in mind. Quickly the price dropped even lower than it had been before. The investor did recoup his losses, but did not make any money on the investment, even though he had held it for over a year and a half.

This was an unusual experience with Tarot cards, and the emotional stress of the querent was clearly visible in the cards. Although my interpretation was accurate, I still feel that Tarot cards are an inappropriate tool for stock picking.

Many investors are now using astrology for this purpose and there is indeed a lot of research into *the stock market and the stars*. However, while planetary transits can be very helpful in determining stock market trends, this should never supersede good old fashioned practical research into the financial condition of the company.

Can you read for someone who is far away? Of course you can read for someone who is not in your presence. What about all those psychic hotlines? And nowadays, people are giving readings on the Internet. However there is one major problem with this. Absentee readings, for many Tarot readers and psychics, can be extremely draining and tiring. Certainly they are for me and other professionals I know. Although why is not understood.

A voice is a vibration that can be picked up on. Nevertheless I will give a Tarot phone reading only to someone who is an established client. I feel I have not made a psychic connection unless I have actually met with someone and given at least one *person-to-person* reading. But I will not read for a *new* client whom I have never seen. This is *my* personal style.

Many Tarot card readers have great success with absentee readings. This is another issue you are going to have to experiment with. Meditating on the querent before the reading, absentee or in person, is quite helpful with the tune-in.

When reading Tarot cards, should a glass of water be set on the table to protect against negative energies? This is a practice I have heard of but I've never actually seen anyone doing it. The theory is that the water absorbs any negative energies that may be floating around or emitting from the querent. Water is the psychic element and symbolic of the subconscious mind. So this may indeed have some validity.

Personally, I think it is more important to *drink* water or other fluids when reading. Psychic readings can be very draining and fluids may help keep your energy up. Some people say the fluids keep the aura clear.

I do encourage you to try different techniques to see what works for you. The glass of water may very well be a useful adjunct to *your* Tarot readings. Another suggestion is to burn incense. The smoke is supposed to have a calming effect on the environment and this makes it easier to center yourself and tune in.

Do you have to believe in Tarot cards for them work? Indeed, belief is very powerful, but Tarot cards work whether or not you believe in them. However, it is pointless to try to learn to read Tarot cards if you do not have an open mind. Your rational mind and intuitive mind will fight with each other like cats and dogs and little or no progress will be made. In order to interpret the Tarot's symbolism, you must develop a rapport with the cards. If you keep thinking that there is nothing to them, you will never be able to make that connection.

On the other hand, if you want to have a Tarot reading—no, you definitely *don't* have to believe in them. Your reading can still be very accurate! I encounter this many times with men. They rarely *believe* in the intuitive arts. However I have read for many staunch disbelievers at parties and, ultimately, they have had to concede that the reading was totally insightful. Some of them even became believers!

When can I become a professional Tarot card reader? Hold your horses! No rush! These things take time. Besides, *being a psychic* [Tarot card reader] *is an endless, glamourless, thankless job; but somebody has to do it.* Actually that was a line made famous by *Dragnet's* Detective Joe Friday. He used to say, "You know that being a policeman is an endless, glamourless, thankless job that's gotta' be done." I've revamped it to describe what it's really like when you hang out your shingle. It's not at all what you'd expect.

People come to you with a myriad of problems. Troubled and distraught, they look for comfort and understanding and often want only to vent about a problem. At times you may feel more like an inexpensive psychiatrist. The release of emotion definitely has a healing effect, and being a good listener is a part of the job. Knowing the future then becomes incidental.

Future-telling is very easy. Dealing with complex human emotions is a huge challenge; and that is really what a professional Tarot card reader does. It is an overwhelming responsibility. I was totally unprepared.

Other times you may feel like a whipping boy because you will also be consulted by people with extremely deep-rooted anger issues. In this case, you cannot be of any service. Venting I allow but *no* fighting with the psychic. Fighting should be done with a psychiatrist.

On occasion I have suggested a therapist, clergyman, physician, or even an accountant be consulted. When one's life is totally out of control, a psychic should not be consulted. As times are now more uncertain and chaotic than ever in our human history, and people are growing unhappier by the day, I have found it necessary to carefully screen all new inquiries for a Tarot card reading. Often their expectations are totally unrealistic.

Reading at psychic fairs and fund-raisers are great ways to learn. (By the way, a psychic fair is great training ground. The pressure is on and you have to learn *fast!*) Along with that, I recommend getting several years of life experience under your belt to enhance the perception of your Tarot card readings, continue reading spiritual literature, and bone-up on basic psychology.

Although a practice could supplement your income, in today's economy you will never be able to earn enough to live comfortably unless giving several sessions a day. But this can cause a severe emotional drain and quickly lead to complete *burn-out*. Furthermore if the pressure is on to pay the bills and this is the sole source of revenue, you may be inclined to compromise quality for quantity.

If you are still interested in an unconventional *job that's gotta' be done*, try taking out an ad in a small local paper or a school newspaper. Business cards can be printed up at a neighborhood printer, with your phone number only, or else people will be stopping by without an appointment demanding instant readings.

Always be tactful, gentle, sensitive, and nonjudgmental. Never tell anyone what to do! Never give advice. Point out the choices that can be made and encourage people to make positive changes in their lives.

You will hear people's most intimate and personal secrets; hence, the consultation and what is heard during it are totally confidential. The querent's privacy is to be completely re-spected.

A Tarot card reading should be a spiritual healing. After-wards the querent should feel optimistic about facing life's chal-lenges.

ANY MORE HELPFUL HINTS?

■ Here is one I got directly from Richard Gardner. He was the famous Tarot expert in England. I had the honor of con-sulting him in London during the summer of 1971. Sadly, it was during the writing of this book that I learned he had passed on. But Richard Gardner's Tarot inspiration will live forever. Al-though he told me this personally, it is also mentioned in his book *The Tarot Speaks*.

Before beginning a reading, separate the cards into piles of their respective suits. The easiest way to do this is to make five different piles: one for Pentacles, one for Cups, one for Wands, one for Swords, and one for the Major Trumps. It is *not* necessary to put them into numerical order, just separat-ing the suits is enough. Join the piles by placing the Major Trumps on the bottom, the Pentacles on top of that, then the Cups, the Wands, and then the Swords. This is the order in which the elements symbolized by the suits fall: 1—earth/Penta-cles; 2—water/Cups; 3— fire/ Wands; 4—air /Swords. However some people feel that the Major Trumps should be placed on top of the pile after the Swords. Again, your personal style.

The purpose of this separation is so that the new querent will not pick up anything from the previous querent (i.e., the previous querent's good or bad luck). This literally *clears the deck.* Plus I find that by doing this one or two suits may predominate (even after the querent has shuffled well) and this helps to zero in on the matters at hand.

If you do more than one spread for a querent, it is *not* necessary to repeat this separating procedure for each spread. Once in the beginning is enough. After that, the querent's vibes will be in the cards.

For those of you who read at parties and special events, as I do, this procedure is much too time-consuming to do for each person. So I suggest doing this only for private, in-depth readings.

▪ Take note of the predominating suits in a spread. This is usually indicative of the main theme of the reading. Several Cups, the issue is love or relationships; Cups and Swords, love and stress; Pentacles and Wands, money and work.

▪ *Look at the cards and say what you see.* Say what you see, not what you think. *No thinking allowed!* In the introduction to Eugen Herrigel's *Zen in the Art of Archery*, Daisetz T. Suzuki says: "As soon as we reflect, deliberate and conceptualize, the original unconsciousness is lost and a thought interferes." In other words, *thinking interferes* and by doing so one can lose the connection to the subconscious mind. That is why I urge you to be spontaneous. Let it flow. Look at the pictures and say what comes to your mind.

Suzuki also talks about *childlikeness.* "*Childlikeness* has to be restored. . . ." Be childlike when looking at the symbols. Allow them to play on your subconscious mind. Make up a story about what you see. You will be surprised at how accurate you are.

When you look at the entire spread, if an impression

bounces up off the cards, go with it—even if it seems illogical. When you transcend logic, you automatically tap into your intuition. Go with what you feel.

■ If the reading seems vague and unclear, focus on the tangible positions: the future, home, the outcome. Then build on that. If you still see confusion, be frank with the querent. She could have many things happening in her life and actually *be* confused about issues. Ask her to reshuffle the cards. If confusion still continues, wait twenty-four hours. Then do another reading.

■ If you get stuck, cover a card with your hand, close your eyes, clear your mind, take a deep breath, and relax. Go with the impressions that immediately come to your mind.

■ Always trust what you see in the cards, even if the querent disagrees. I cannot count the many times I have made a prediction and the querent would swear it was an impossibility. In a few days, weeks, or months, I'd get a call telling me it happened exactly as I had said. Always go with what you see or feel.

If you feel you are not *connecting*, continue to follow your intuition, regardless. Years ago, I used to work at parties for sophisticated Park Avenue socialites, ladies who lunch. I remember my cronies and I would think we were not connecting because they (the socialites) would stare at us blankly, giving us absolutely no *facial* feedback. (This was the face-lift crowd.) Once I complained to the hostess about the lack of reaction from her guests. Her answer: "They think they're above it. They're raving about the readings!"

The moral of this story is, regardless of lack of feedback, go with what you see or feel. One exception, however, is if the querent's eyebrows are raised high on her forehead; maybe then you *should* reorient your reading.

■ Always keep an open mind when you look into someone's cards. You never know what you'll see. *Never judge a book by its cover. Things aren't always what they seem to be.* Don't be surprised by anything.

■ Experiment. Try different spreads and different techniques. See what works for you. Put your style and personality into your method.

■ And another reminder: Take *dated* notes of the cards that come up in the readings.

What if I have more questions? If you have more questions, my web site is www.wilmacarroll.com. My e-mail address is wilma.carroll@verizon.net. I will endeavor to answer all inquiries.

IV

THE SEVEN TRIPLETS OR
THE SEVEN SISTERS SPREAD

The Legacy of Polly's Tea Room

Many years ago, I used to visit an elderly European woman who read in a Philadelphia tea room. The Countess, as she was known, had lived a life that rivaled the drama of a Verdi opera combined with the excitement of a James Bond film. She had been a spy during World War II, had seen a close friend killed by the enemy, and claimed her mother had helped found the famed L'Institute de Métaphysiques in Paris.

Highly spiritual and a powerful clairvoyant, the Countess used playing cards, not Tarot cards. I would watch her closely as she skillfully laid out the cards in the Seven Triplets Spread. Her accuracy and her insight were my inspiration.

Although this spread was designed for reading with playing cards, I have adapted it for the Tarot. This is a slightly more advanced exercise. It teaches how more detailed information can be gleaned from a spread by using more cards, reading *surrounding* cards and noting the predominating suit or suits. It also prepares you for the more complex spreads. The Seven Triplets Spread uses twenty-one cards in groups of threes (See Diagram 4.1).

1. Shuffle and cut the cards as usual and then lay them out faceup following Diagram 4.1. Make one pile at a time of three cards going from left to right. *Pay attention to the cards as you lay them out! Now is the time to start getting your nose out of the book and into these cards.*

2. Take a quick note of the predominating suit or suits in the spread, if any.

3. Focus on the center or middle card of each pile.

4. After a quick focus on the center card, note the cards surrounding the center card, the card to the right of the center card, and the card to the left of the center card. These add to the interpretation.

5. The surrounding cards can be interpreted as influences around the center card or actual events or people. They add more information. This is very similar to the first exercise, the E-Z Three Card Spread. Each card adds a bit of information to the interpretation.

When looking at the three cards, note if there is a symbol in one card, that reminds you of a symbol in the other card. Look for a similar theme in each card, then link them. It's like playing *connect the dots*.

6. If one of the surrounding cards appears to be more outstanding than the center card, go with your intuition and focus on what hits you as the strongest. Go with what pulls you

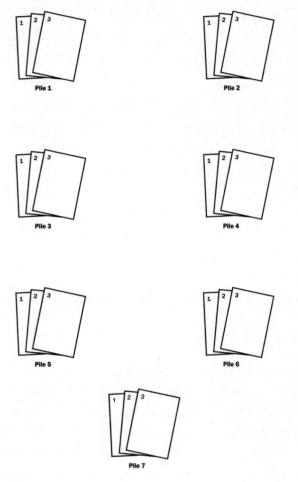

DIAGRAM 4.1

Seven Triplets or Seven Sisters Spread

in immediately. If only two of the cards strike you, giving clear information, go with that and disregard the other card.

7. Let your imagination play with the images. This generates the intuition. *Look at the cards and say what you see*; and incorporate that with the trade secret: Look at the *overall picture(s)*.

Let's look at a sample pile (See Diagram 4.2). The 3 of Wands, The World, the 6 of Swords. The World is the center card, so the focus could be travel. The 3 of Wands to the left could be business at a distance. The 6 of Swords to the right could be travel by boat or by air (Swords are symbolic of the *air* element). Tying it all together, distant travel for business by boat or air over water (an airplane flying over water). This is one of the many possible interpretations. It is ultimately up to *your* intuition.

Let's look at a sample of an entire Seven Sisters Spread. This

DIAGRAM 4.2

Sample Pile of Seven Triplets Spread

reading was given to Peggy. A young woman of twenty-six years, she was already on her way up the corporate ladder.

Lay the cards out accordingly, then follow along with the interpretation.

Pile 1—From left to right—8 of Pentacles, The Star, 2 of Pentacles.

Pile 2—From left to right—4 of Wands, Death, 10 of Pentacles.

Pile 3—From left to right—6 of Cups, The Hanged Man, 10 of Wands.

Pile 4—From left to right—7 of Pentacles, Ace of Pentacles, 6 of Pentacles.

Pile 5—From left to right—Queen of Swords, The Empress, Knight of Swords.

Pile 6—From left to right—The Tower, Wheel of Fortune, The Fool.

Pile 7—From left to right—6 of Wands, Judgement, 8 of Wands.

Now for the interpretation. A quick overview of the cards shows all the suits are represented. There does not appear to be one suit in particular that predominates. This immediately says that there may be several themes going on here.

Returning to Pile 1: I find The Star in the middle is the focus. This could mean recognition; the 8 of Pentacles, work or recognition in work; the 2 of Pentacles, a little more money comes with the recognition. This could be interpreted as a promotion in work, with an increase in salary.

Moving to Pile 2: I am following my intuition on this one, connecting the dots. The first pile spoke of a promotion. The 4 of Wands could be an office. But the Death card says it's *new*, and the 10 of Pentacles adds a *plush* flavor to it. With a promotion, logically, can come a new and nicer office.

Looking at Pile 3: This looks like an entirely different theme to me. The 6 of Cups is a friend, but the 10 of Wands is heavy responsibility. The Hanged Man is a martyr. My interpretation is that a friend of Peggy's cries excessively on her shoulder. Peggy may feel overburdened and taken advantage of in this friendship.

On to Pile 4: The Pentacles are, obviously, money. My intuition tells me this relates to the very first theme (Pile 1) about getting a raise. My interpretation is that Peggy is contemplating making some investments per the 7 of Pentacles. The Ace of Pentacles indicates perhaps real estate investments or long-term secure investments. The 6 of Pentacles shows she is talking to someone about financial advice.

Down to Pile 5: This looks like another very different theme. The Empress in the center hits me strongly as Peggy's mother. The Knight of Swords tells of an argument with her mother. The Queen of Swords adds to the description of the mother, which is *difficult*. Peggy heartily agreed.

Over to Pile 6: The Wheel of Fortune pulls me in first. The Tower indicates the unexpected. The Fool can indicate *risky business*. I am uncertain how to concretely interpret this. But I *feel* it augurs something lucky and unexpected. That is as far I can *see* with this pile. Nevertheless I *say what I see*, even if it is *symbolically speaking* and not necessarily specific; eventually it will make sense.

At the bottom is Pile 7: I predict a lot of paperwork and messages awaiting Peggy when she gets back to her office.

At the conclusion of the reading, Peggy confirmed the insights. She had gotten a promotion with a substantial increase in salary. This also came with a new office. Not a corner office, but two doors down from one. That brought her closer to the corporate power structure. She also had an upcoming meeting with a financial advisor in order to do some long-term financial planning.

Peggy admitted to feeling taken advantage of by a childhood friend who constantly cried on her shoulder. And a recent argument with her mother had been unsettling. Peggy feared another confrontation.

When she returned to her office, there were mounds of contracts on her desk awaiting her approval. Peggy called me to complain vehemently about that. She was angry because it was accurate. Sometimes you actually get blamed for *accuracy*! *Being a psychic is a thankless job.* . . .

Later that evening Peggy called again. She had forgotten about a lottery ticket purchased early that day, a risk *practical* Peggy never before had taken. She won $100!

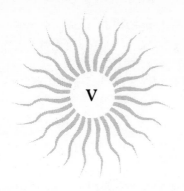

THE INFORMATION
SUPER HIGHWAY

ADVANCED SPREADS AND LITTLE EXTRAS

"I need more information!" cried Ronnie.

A high school senior, Ronnie began reading Tarot cards in her sophomore year. Working only with the basic Celtic Cross Spread, she frequently gave readings to her friends, having earned a reputation for incredible accuracy.

As she prepared to participate in a fundraiser for her class graduation party, Ronnie told me she wanted to get more information from the cards.

Indeed lots of extra information can be seen in the advanced spreads. There are hundreds of sophisticated and unusual spreads that have survived the ages. Remember, which ones you use depend on your data needs, time constraints, and personal taste. Here are several I have collected over the years.

THE *ADVANCED* CELTIC CROSS SPREAD

1. Shuffle and cut the cards as usual. Then lay them out in the traditional Celtic Cross Spread.

2. Go to Position 6 which represents the future (before you) and place another card to the right of the card that is already there. Go to Position 7 (you) and place another card to the right of the card in that position. Do the same with Position 8 (home, friends, and environment) and position 10 (culmination).

3. Return again to Position 6 and place another card to the right of the two cards already there. You now have three cards in that position. Repeat the same procedure in Positions 7, 8, and 10 (See Diagram 5.1).

You now have the Celtic Cross Spread with a touch of the Seven Sisters Spread.

Interpret the cards in the groups of three by focusing on the center card first (or whichever card strikes you as the strongest), then the two surrounding cards. Project what you see in those cards into the positions in which they fall. Keep in mind, the cards themselves ultimately transcend the positions in which they fall. If you have difficulty remembering the meanings of the spreads' positions, focus only on the cards. Here again, the same rules of interpretation apply: *Look at the cards and say what you see.* Try to go for the *overall picture(s)*. Be spontaneous. Do not get caught up in *thinking*. If you get a *feel-*

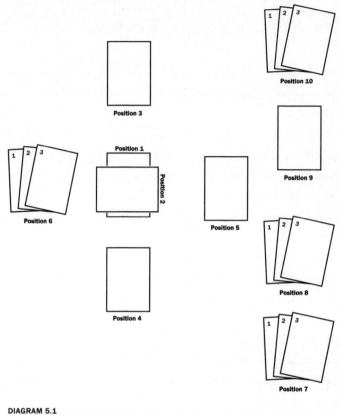

DIAGRAM 5.1

Advanced Celtic Cross Spread

ing by looking at the cards, no matter how irrational, go with it. In fact, by now you are probably learning to *feel* the cards. Go with the feeling.

Some Tarot readers suggest that you build the three groups of cards for *every* position in the spread. Personally, I do not like this procedure. I think it is easier to put the emphasis on the more tangible positions. However, feel free to experiment and see what works for you.

THE HOROSCOPE SPREAD

The Horoscope Spread is actually based on the astrological horoscope. The positions in this spread correspond with the interpretations of the houses of the horoscope. The houses of the horoscope represent areas of life.

Starting from the left side going counterclockwise, make a circle with twelve cards (See Diagram 5.2). Place a 13th card in the center of the spread.

Interpret the cards in the context of the meanings of the houses in which they fall. These meanings could fill a book. Here, I am giving you very concise explanations with sample interpretations. For more in-depth analyses, a book on basic astrology is useful.

FIRST HOUSE—The personality of the querent, the environment or how others see the querent, appearance or image that is projected to the world, the beginning of a matter. For example, the 5 of Wands in this position may mean the querent is competitive or athletic, or others see the querent as manipulative. The Page of Swords in this position may mean the querent has a bad temper or is impulsive.

SECOND HOUSE—Money, possessions, earning power, financial affairs, values, and the querent's sense of self-worth. The 9 of Pentacles in this position may mean the querent has expensive tastes, or is a high-maintenance woman.

THIRD HOUSE—Neighbors, neighborhoods, relatives, siblings, day-to-day activities, communications, short journeys, mes-

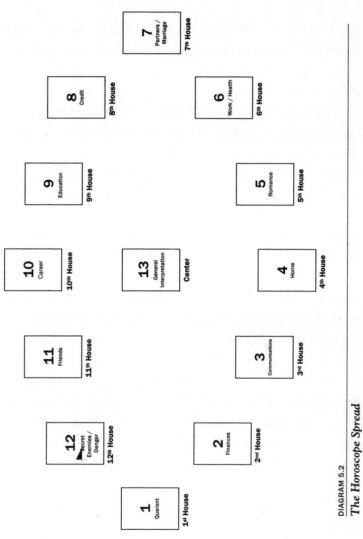

DIAGRAM 5.2
The Horoscope Spread

sages, phone calls, and gossip. The 7 of Swords in this position may mean a thief or robberies in the neighborhood.

FOURTH HOUSE—Home, family, father, the end of the matter. The 8 of Pentacles in this position may mean repair work being done in the home.

FIFTH HOUSE—Romance, love affairs, children, pregnancy, vacations, games and amusements, self-expression, creativity, artistic ability, investments, gambling, speculation, and cats. The Hermit in this position may mean looking for love (in all the wrong places). The High Priestess here may mean a secret lover.

SIXTH HOUSE—Health, work, pets (except cats), employees, tenants, servants, uncles, aunts. The Moon in this position may mean a health condition or upset stomach caused by stress. In astrology the moon symbolizes emotional needs. In the Horoscope Spread, The Moon (and/or The Sun) intensifies the position in which it falls. Therefore, this could mean that the health and emotional state of the querent are in some way intertwined.

SEVENTH HOUSE—Partners (personal and/or professional), spouse, marriage, business contacts, clients, open enemies, agents, grandparents, outcome of legal matters, legal advice, lawyers. The Knight of Swords in this position may mean an argumentative spouse or client or an argument with a partner. The 4 of Cups falling here may mean a *fantasy* relationship.

EIGHTH HOUSE—Manner of death, sex, taxes, other people's money, credit, insurance, partner's money, inheritances, wills, surgery, values, spiritual rebirth, psychotherapy. The 6 of Pentacles in this position may mean talking to someone about borrowing money. The 6 of Cups in this house may mean a relationship based on mutually shared values.

NINTH HOUSE—Education, travel, long distance journeys, foreign countries, legal matters, law, science, psychology, publishing, horses, the clergy, the church or religious institutions, grandchildren, in-laws, higher mind activities (spirituality, philosophy, religion). The Sun in this position may mean education gives the querent a feeling of confidence. In astrology, the sun symbolizes the ego. Remember, when falling in any position in this spread, The Sun (and/or The Moon) intensifies the significance. For the querent, perhaps education and the ego are in some way intertwined. This is where the querent shines!

TENTH HOUSE—Career, profession, fame, reputation, employer, judges, mother. The Star in this position may mean recognition in career. The Ace of Cups in this house may mean a message about a new job opportunity.

ELEVENTH HOUSE—Friends, acquaintances, groups of people, clubs, organizations, stepchildren, foster children, adopted children, money from career, hopes and wishes. The 4 of Wands in this position may mean visiting the home of friends. The World falling here may mean a friend who is a foreigner.

TWELFTH HOUSE—Secret enemies, hidden dangers, the subconscious, confinement (prisons, hospitals, mental institutions), restrictions, self-undoing, seclusion, behind-the-scenes manipulation. The 8 of Swords in this position may mean imprisonment.

THE CENTER CARD/THE THIRTEENTH CARD IN THE MIDDLE—
This card can have a very general interpretation. It can be read
as the outcome of the situation, the card that ties everything
together, or it merely adds more information to the reading. To
get the most out of it, *look at the card and say what you see.*

The Horoscope Spread gives an enormous amount of information. While I have been preaching how *non-formulaic* a
Tarot card reading is, with this spread you are going to go card-
by-card, position-by-position. Because these positions are so
significant, this spread may tend to be a little formulaic. Nevertheless the same rules of intuition still apply here as well. If you
get a *feeling* from the *overall picture(s)*, go with it! And, remember to *look at the cards and say what you see.* Plus another reminder for interpretative purposes is that The Sun and/or The
Moon falling in this spread intensifies the importance of the
house in which it falls.

Let's look at a sample of the Horoscope Spread. Lauren gave
this reading to her neighbor Marianne. Lauren could tell that
Marianne was upset about something. After the reading, she
understood why. Lay the cards out accordingly in the appropri-
ate positions. Remember, focus on the cards as you lay them out
and then follow along with the interpretation.

First House—Knight of Pentacles
Second House—8 of Cups
Third House—Ace of Swords
Fourth House—The Lovers
Fifth House—6 of Cups
Sixth House—The World
Seventh House—7 of Cups

Eighth House—5 of Cups
Ninth House—Queen of Pentacles
Tenth House—The Chariot
Eleventh House—5 of Pentacles
Twelfth House—7 of Swords
Center Card/The 13th Card in the Middle—2 of Cups

With the cards in front of you, note how Lauren interpreted the Horoscope Spread. Starting at the First House, follow along sequentially around the circle.

First House—Knight of Pentacles—A man was around Marianne. In other words, a man was *in the picture.*

Second House—8 of Cups—Marianne was clearly turning away from something. But this was the house of money, and Cups represent emotion. However the Second House also tells about one's values. Lauren's interpretation was quite astute. She concluded that Marianne was turning away from something that was *emotionally empty and unfulfilling.* At the time, Lauren had no idea what she was talking about. That happens many times when giving a reading. You are reading symbols and they don't make sense. Go with what you see, and that is exactly what Lauren did.

Third House—Ace of Swords—An e-mail awaited Marianne. The Third House symbolizes communications.

Fourth House—The Lovers—Love comes to Marianne's house. Silently Lauren thought to herself, this reading was getting very interesting and definitely had something to do with a love problem; although at that moment Lauren had no idea where it was going. She proceeded by looking at the cards and saying what she saw.

Fifth House—6 of Cups—The card of friendship in the

house of romance. Lauren had no idea how to interpret this. So she simply stated what she was seeing, a friendship and romance.

Sixth House—The World—Here again, Lauren isn't sure what it means, so she reads it as she sees it: travel and work.

Seventh House—7 of Cups—Confusion in a relationship.

Eighth House—5 of Cups—Lauren is uncertain how to interpret this card in the context of the meaning of the Eighth House. This is the most complex astrological house because it deals with deep transformation. Lauren goes with her intuition, looks at the card and says what she sees. There is an *emotional loss.*

Ninth House—Queen of Pentacles—Lauren tells Marianne she will learn new things about computers. The Ninth House deals with learning and education.

Tenth House—The Chariot—Marianne is moving forward with her career. While this is a positive indication for Marianne's career, because of the other cards in the spread, Lauren knows all is not well.

Eleventh House—5 of Pentacles—This is the house of friends. Lauren suggests that Marianne may feel that a friendship has no value.

Twelfth House—7 of Swords—This really throws Lauren off. The Twelfth House is the house of hidden or secret matters. The card indicates something *sneaky.* Lauren tactfully says what she sees.

The Center Card/The 13th Card in the Middle—2 of Cups—Lauren sums up the reading by stating there is a romantic relationship in progress!

Afterwards Marianne confirmed what was going on. She had just started a job in a travel agency, was learning a lot about computers, and advancing careerwise. That aspect of her life was working well.

However, she did have serious emotional conflicts because of a *perplexing* relationship matter. Her best friend's boyfriend had been pursuing *her*. In fact, he frequently stopped by Marianne's house and constantly e-mailed her. But Marianne wanted to be loyal to her best friend. She thought the loss of her friend would bring more pain than the gain of her best friend's boyfriend.

Marianne confessed to having an attraction to this guy, but grappled with the loyalty issue. At other times she vacillated and was uncertain if the friendship was even worth it, regardless of the boyfriend issue. She confided to Lauren that she and the boyfriend had gone out three times and sneaked off to out-of-the-way places so as not to be noticed.

Lauren predicted that Marianne would ultimately have a clandestine relationship with this guy. She did. It lasted for several months, unbeknownst to Marianne's best friend, then quietly fizzled out.

The Horoscope Spread can also be used to answer a specific question. In astrology, this is known as *horary astrology*. It is a highly specialized technique. A chart is drawn up to answer a specific question based on the time it is asked (of the hour).

When applying this technique to the (Tarot) Horoscope Spread, each house will give information relating to the question. Or you can refer solely to the houses that pertain directly to the question and disregard the others.

The best example is a specific question about *love*, which this spread is particularly effective in answering. To ask if you will have a relationship with a certain individual or the status of a current relationship, refer to the First House (you or your environment), Fifth House (the house of romance) and/or the Seventh House (the house of relationships).

To be even more precise, identify the intended's significator first. For instance, if you are interested in a dark-haired man, twenty-two years old, select the Knight of Pentacles. However, *keep it in the deck.* Then pose the question clearly. *Will I have a romance (or relationship) with this person?* Shuffle, cut, and then deal out the spread. If the Knight of Pentacles (or the desired individual's significator) appears in the First House, he is definitely around you and on the scene; in the Fifth House or the Seventh House is also confirmation something is happening. In the Fourth House, he is in your home. In the Sixth House, maybe he works with you. In the Eleventh House, he is a *friend* and nothing much will happen beyond that.

If you want more information from the Horoscope Spread, the following is an advanced version. It can also be used to answer a specific question, while adding more details.

THE *ADVANCED* HOROSCOPE SPREAD

The Advanced Horoscope Spread involves groups of three as previously learned. Beginning with the basic Horoscope Spread of one card for each position, return to the first card in the First House. Start again at the first card and lay another card down to the right of the first card and continue doing so in each position. Go around the spread for a third time, ending with three cards in each position including the center/middle position (See Diagram 5.3). This is the Advanced Horoscope Spread. It is the Horoscope Spread with a taste of the Seven Sisters Spread.

The same rules of interpretation apply. Focus on the middle

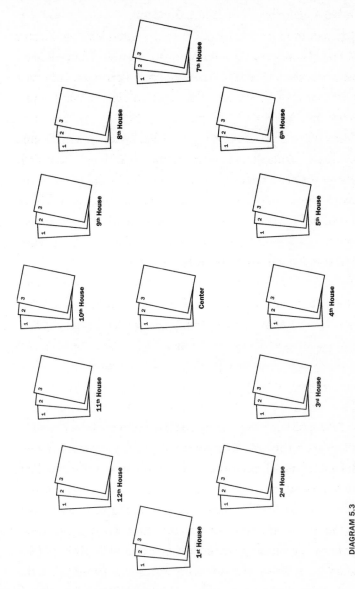

DIAGRAM 5.3

Advanced Horoscope Spread

card or the most outstanding in the pile. *Look at the cards and say what you see.* Be spontaneous. Remember, *your first hunch is usually your best!*

When asking a specific question with this spread, it will give more in-depth information than the basic Horoscope Spread.

FIVE-BY-FIVE (MONTH-BY-MONTH) SPREAD

The Five-By-Five Spread is presented with the compliments of Lynn M. Buess, author of *The Tarot and Transformation.* I have renamed it the Month-By-Month Spread. This is excellent for *future-telling.* Begin by shuffling and cutting the cards as usual. Starting at the left, place five cards in a row going from left to right.

Above that row, going from left to right, lay down another five cards in a row. Continue this three more times making a total of five rows of five cards each (See Diagram 5.4). By the way, these directions can be altered to go from right to left if that suits you as a reader

The bottom row describes the past or immediate past. The next to the bottom row is the present. The row above that, the middle row, is the following month. The fourth row is the next month after that. And the fifth row projects three to five months thereafter.

The focus can be the center card of each row with the surrounding cards adding more information. If the center card does not strike you as the most significant, go with what you *feel* or what grabs your attention first. Another tip: interpret the cards that clearly resonate with you. If some do not make sense, skip over them. Do not pause to think. Be spontaneous. These

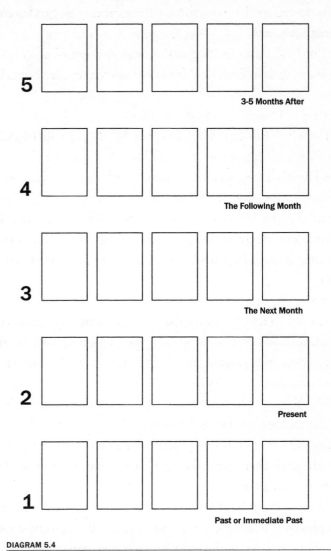

5   3-5 Months After

4   The Following Month

3   The Next Month

2   Present

1   Past or Immediate Past

DIAGRAM 5.4

Five-By-Five (Month-By-Month) Spread

spreads are more complex because you are dealing with more cards. But all of these symbols will be bouncing and waking up your *intuitive/psychic faculties*. Say what comes to your mind instantly. This allows for the flow of energy to easily continue.

Let's look at a sample of the Five-By-Five/Month-By-Month Spread. Noah, fresh out of college and newly employed at a public relations firm, gave this reading in October 2001 to his roommate, Ross. Lay the cards out accordingly and follow along with the interpretation. Pay close attention to the details in the cards. What you see in the cards is really more important than what you see in the book!

> *Row One*—3 of Pentacles, 5 of Wands, 8 of Pentacles, The
>   Magician, and 10 of Pentacles.
> *Row Two*—3 of Cups, 2 of Cups, 9 of Cups, 6 of Cups, and
>   4 of Wands.
> *Row Three*—The Lovers, Death, The Tower, Page of Swords,
>   and Knight of Swords.
> *Row Four*—Knight of Pentacles, The Devil, Knight of Wands,
>   5 of Cups, and Queen of Cups.
> *Row Five*—8 of Wands, The Hermit, The World, 6 of
>   Swords, and 8 of Cups.

This is Noah's interpretation.

Row One: This was the very recent past. Noah saw that Ross had a job that gave him a lot of power. The job centered around exercising. Ross had, in fact, gotten a new job the previous month as the manager of an exclusive health club.

Row Two: This was the present, in the month of October. Ross had a girlfriend he very much cared for. Lisa brought him a lot of joy and happiness. They shared common interests, had many friends, and thought about living together some time down the road.

Row Three: This represents the following month, which would be November. Here Noah is literally projecting into the future. He tells Ross that his old girlfriend will unexpectedly pop up on the scene. The Lovers next to Death, which is next to The Tower. Ross's reaction was that this would be impossible, insisting it would never happen.

This is where being a psychic becomes frustrating. If a querent knows what will *not* happen in the future, then the querent should know what *will* happen in the future and should not be consulting a psychic. Furthermore when a querent starts to disagree, it can shut off the psychic flow. Intense concentration is needed, and the reader should avoid an emotional reaction. Noah kept his focus. To him the message was clear and correct.

He also advised Ross, who was by now in complete denial about this forecast, that Lisa would find out and be furious. Noah remained tactful and gentle and continued the reading.

Row Four: This represents the month following November, which would be December. Noah was still predicting. He told Ross that to further complicate matters, Lisa's old boyfriend would return. Ross will have a jealous and angry reaction. He will be crushed by these turn of events. He will try to win back Lisa's affection by giving her a nice gift (Queen of Cups). It is December, time for Christmas presents. By now, Ross's face had drained of blood. Noah had made a genuine psychic connection. He proceeded.

Row Five: This represents three to five months after December. Noah's focus was on the center card in this row, The World. His prediction: Ross would be so disillusioned with love he would take off and travel far away in search of adventure.

Noah told me Ross sat there staring in motionless disbelief. The next few months revealed how clairvoyant Noah's reading really was. This was how the events transpired.

In November, Ross's old girlfriend joined the health club where he worked. They were seen talking together and someone told Lisa. She went into a rage. In December, Lisa's old boyfriend got in touch with her. He said he missed her. Ross could understand that because Lisa was a wonderful lady and he did not want to lose her. He seethed with jealousy, just as Noah predicted, and bought Lisa an expensive Christmas gift in an attempt to impress her. It didn't work. Obviously, she was no longer *in the picture*.

By mid-February, Ross was *not* a happy camper. He began mumbling about joining the Foreign Legion. Instead, he quit his job and headed for Alaska.

These kinds of clear psychic experiences are very possible with Tarot cards. Noah looked at the cards and responded to his spontaneous feelings. In that way, he accurately projected into the future.

The timing of events can be effectively determined in this spread by calculating the querent's numerological personal months, and interpreting the meaning of those vibrations in the context of the cards that fall in a particular row.

Once you have obtained the querent's *current* personal month, backtrack or count back by one number. This will give you the querent's previous month's vibration or the *last* personal month. Apply the querent's *last* personal month to the bottom row of the spread, which represents the past or immediate past. Apply the querent's *current* personal month to the row above, representing the querent's immediate situation. The numerological vibration for the querent's next personal month is applied to the middle row of cards. It will give you added information of what the querent may expect in that month. Do the same for the following personal month, applying it to the fourth row of cards (the fourth row from the bottom). For the fifth row, which is three to five months into the future, you may have to *feel* which personal month coming up will have the most impact on the querent. Here is where intuition comes in handy. If this is too difficult, simply stick to applying the personal months to the first three or four rows or only the ones which are easy to interpret. Never spend time belaboring something you can't figure out. Move on, continuing with spontaneity.

Meanwhile, let's check out Ross's personal vibes to see how they can be factored into this reading. The calendar year when this reading was given was 2001. The month was October. Ross's birthday is February 3.

Here's a quick refresher for finding the *personal month*. Calculate the *universal year* by adding the digits of the current calendar year or, in this case, the year in which the reading was given (2001). $2 + 0 + 0 + 1 = 3$. The *universal year* is a 3. *Always reduce to a single digit,* if necessary! Calculate the querent's *personal year* by adding his *birth month* and *birth day* to the *universal year.* Ross's birth month is February (2). His birth day is the third (3) of February. The universal year is a 3. $2 + 3 + 3 = 8$. Ross's *personal year* is an 8. *Always reduce to a single digit,* whenever necessary. Calculate his *personal month* by adding his *personal year* to the current *calendar month.* The reading was given in the month of October (10). $8 + 1 + 0 = 9$. *Always reduce to a single digit,* if necessary. In October 2001, Ross was in a 9 *personal month.*

To recap: In 2001 Ross was in an 8 *personal year.* In October (2001), he was in a 9 *personal month.*

Let's start with the bottom row, which represents the immediate past. Since the reading was given in October (when Ross was in a 9 personal month), the previous month, would be September. Ross was in an 8 personal month. However, since he was also in an 8 personal year, there is a *double whammy* of the strong 8 vibration. It fits perfectly! In September, Ross had landed a great job. It paid well (8 is money); gave him some power (8 is power, leadership, and executive ability); and, interestingly enough, 8 is the number of physical exercise.

The second row represents the present, the month when the reading is given. For Ross, it was a 9 personal month. 9 is the number of *romance*, candle light, and music. The cards tell of the happiness with his girlfriend. However, 9 is also the number of endings. This should have sent a *red flag* up in Noah's mind.

The next row, the third, indicating the following month, November, speaks of *things to come*. Ross moved into a *1* personal month, a time of new beginnings. This is where observation of numerological vibrations gives you the experience to interpret these subtle nuances. For Ross, it meant *the beginning of the end* or the beginning of *madness*. Another clue is that he was moving into a 9 personal *year* in 2002, a time of endings. Given that, the trouble with Lisa was probably inevitable. Yet it *began* in November.

Going to the fourth row, December, Ross was in an *1½* personal month, a time of stress. Ross had lost the woman he loved.

The last row indicated the next few months. However, by this time, Ross was in a completely different personal year vibration, the ending vibe, 9. And, that is certainly what happened. (Remember a personal year can indicate major life transitions.) Ross's relationship had ended, and he ended his great job. A 9 year can also indicate globe-trotting. Ross took off in February 2002, an $1\frac{1}{2}$ personal month, a time of stress. You could easily say, per these vibes, Ross was running away.

Again, intuition and experience will make interpreting the numerological vibrations very easy. Start observing your personal vibrations and those of your friends and family. You will be amazed by the insights you get!

ONE-YEAR SPREAD

This is an excellent spread that gives you a quick overview of an entire year. It consists of twelve cards (plus a significator). Each card represents a month in the year. It is exceptionally effective when incorporating the querent's personal months into the interpretation, and it is very apropos at the beginning of the New Year. It can still be used at any time, but it always begins with the current calendar month. So, if you give this reading in August, that month would mark the beginning of the spread. In other words, the first position or first card of this spread would be read as August. The second position or second card would be September, and so on.

Aesthetically, the pattern of this spread does require a significator. Choose one that you view as representative of the querent. Place it in the middle (See Diagram 5.5). Then, starting at the top towards the left, while moving downward, diagonally towards the right, lay out six cards. Follow the same procedure, starting at the top towards the right. Lay out six cards moving downward, diagonally towards the left. You should now have a cross with the significator in the middle. The first card is read as January or the current calendar month; the second card is read

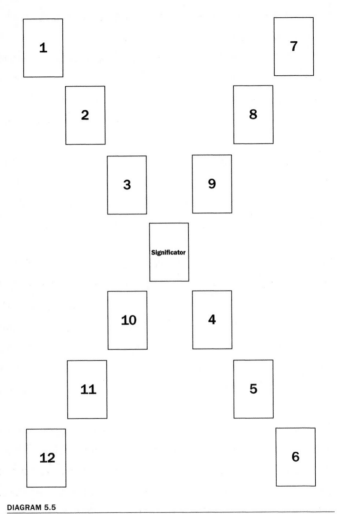

DIAGRAM 5.5

One-Year Spread

as February or the next month. After reading that diagonal row, start at the top of the other diagonal row and read that card as the seventh month all the way down to the last card, which is the last month or December.

Let's look at a sample of this spread, while also incorporating the querent's personal months. This reading was given to Joshua, a graduate of a prestigious midwestern university. Joshua had graduated three years earlier with a degree in political science. After college, he and two friends migrated to Colorado, attempting to open a restaurant. It was a dismal failure; so, with his tail between his legs, Josh returned to his hometown of Jacksonville, Florida, to be close to his large family. At the time of this reading he was managing a trendy Cajun restaurant.

Josh's birthday is July 22. The reading was given in 1999.

Here's another formula refresher for finding the *personal month*. Calculate the *universal year* by adding the digits of the current *calendar year. Always reduce to a single digit!* Calculate the querent's *personal year* by adding his *birth month* and *birth day* to the *universal year. Always reduce to a single digit!* Calculate his *personal month* by adding his *personal year* to the current *calendar month. Always reduce to a single digit!*

At the beginning of the New Year (1999), Josh had entered a 3 personal year. Based on that information, by backtracking, I easily calculated that the previous year (the entire *calendar* year of 1998) he was in an $1\frac{1}{2}$ personal year, meaning it was stressful. (It always helps to take note of where someone is coming from, because that helps to understand where one is going. This is how basic numerology helps to *ground* a psychic/Tarot reading!) A 3 personal year is much lighter and easier going. Since the reading was given to him in very early January, the first card represents the month of January. It is also a 4 personal month for Josh.

Lay the cards out accordingly, noticing the details in the pictures. Try first to read this spread *without* looking in the book. This will give you the opportunity to gradually start easing your nose *out* of the book. Then follow along with my interpretation and compare that with your interpretation. Remember, these interpretations are not written in stone; so don't be disappointed if you come up with something different from what I am suggesting.

Significator—Knight of Cups (I deemed this card as befitting of Joshua because he has blond hair and blue eyes.)

Position 1—January—8 of Pentacles.
Position 2—February—The World.
Position 3—March—3 of Cups.
Position 4—April—4 of Swords.
Position 5—May—Wheel of Fortune.
Position 6—June—2 of Cups.
Position 7—July—The Lovers.
Position 8—August—5 of Cups.
Position 9—September—7 of Wands.
Position 10—October—7 of Cups.
Position 11—November—10 of Wands.
Position 12—December—6 of Swords.

Here is the interpretation. I am looking at the cards, and interpreting each card as one month of the year. But this time the numerological vibration of the querent's personal month is going to be woven into making the prediction.

Position 1—a 4 personal month: The 8 of Pentacles shows a

man working. *4* is the number of work. I told Joshua he would be hard at work in this month. See how easily it fits!

Position 2—a 5 personal month: The World is obviously long distance travel. The 5 may also indicate travel, as well as *the unexpected*. I informed Joshua that he would probably take an *unexpected* vacation in February. Of course he disagreed.

Position 3—a 6 personal month: The 3 of Cups looks like a festive event. 6 is the number of family. A festive family function. I predicted there would be a joyous family party.

Position 4—a 7 personal month: The 4 of Swords looks as if someone is sleeping or taking a long rest. A 7 personal month, in general, indicates the time to rest and restore energy. When this vibration is in effect, many people do not even feel like going out. Instead they stay home and take frequent naps. Or they sit and stare at the television, without even paying attention to what they are watching. This is a heavy *thinking* time. I suggested in April Josh would have to slow down, rest up, and *recharge his battery*.

Position 5—an 8 personal month: The Wheel of Fortune is luck. 8 is money. Clearly, this looked like luck with money.

Position 6—a 9 personal month: The 2 of Cups is a relationship; but, 9 is a time of endings. And that is exactly what it looked like—the *ending* of a relationship. I eased into this one because it is sensitive. However Joshua did confide that the relationship with his girlfriend was dicey and a breakup would not surprise him.

Position 7—a 1 personal month: The Lovers is a Major Trump card. That indicates something immediate. *1* is the time of *new* beginnings. Upon seeing this, I advised Joshua that all was not lost. Immediately following the break-up, a new summer romance would quickly heat up July.

Position 8—an $1\frac{1}{2}$ personal month: The figure in the 5 of Cups does not look happy. Three cups are overturned. Something is spilled out or lost. And, an $1\frac{1}{2}$ personal month can be stressful. This card may indicate disappointment. Plus, it *follows* The Lovers. My intuition told me to stay with the love theme. I predicted a souring of the sizzling summer *love story*.

Position 9—a 3 personal month: The 7 of Wands speaks of power struggles. But 3 is the vibration of friends. Perhaps there will be power struggles with friends.

Position 10—a 4 personal month: The 7 of Cups shows someone who can't make up his mind. As 4 is the number of work, I advised Joshua that October would probably be a time of confusion and indecisiveness regarding work and career matters.

Position 11—a 5 personal month: This guy is carrying a heavy load. The 10 of Wands speaks of being laden down with responsibility. Add the 5 for a dose of *expect the unexpected*. It was, in my estimation, an *unexpected* overload of burdens relating to work. Therefore, in November, Josh could expect an *unexpected* addition of duties on the job.

Position 12—a 6 personal month: The 6 of Swords can be an airplane trip or a shorter trip by car along a highway. Since Joshua was in a 6 personal month, which usually means home or nearby related, my intuition told me he was going to travel, but not too far. And, most likely, it would be a trip having to do with family. My prediction was that in December (twelve months from the reading) Joshua would take a car trip to visit family.

Since I knew from numerology that Joshua was moving into a 4 personal year the following year (after the Tarot cards' reading had expired), I added to my predictions that in the next year he would have no choice but to sort out all the work and career issues.

I heard from Joshua about eighteen months later. Here's how it all played out.

He did work very hard during the month of January. He was so exhausted that he impulsively took a vacation in February, just to chill out. In March his cousin got married. There was a big wedding, and family members from several states flew in to attend. Indeed family was the main event of that month. By April, Josh was wiped out again. He used downtime to sleep. In May, his boss the restaurant owner gave Joshua a huge increase in salary. But, in June, Joshua's girlfriend ended their relationship. In July, however, he met a beautiful redhead and fell in love instantly. One month later (August), he concluded, "She was transparent. I could see right through her." He realized beauty was only skin-deep. What a *disappointment*! As September rolled around, Joshua had some conflicts with what he described as *controlling friends*. In October he admitted to himself he was confused about job matters. Maybe the restaurant business wasn't where he should be. It didn't matter, because in November he was hit with even more responsibility. His boss was opening another restaurant. This man trusted Joshua and wanted him to oversee the entire new operation! As the holiday season got going in December, Joshua decided to take a short car journey, about two hours west of Jacksonville, to visit his brother, sister-in-law, and twin nieces. As he had moved into a 4 personal year by the time I heard from him; he told me he was unhappy managing a restaurant, and was indeed taking a serious look at his career direction.

This spread is quick and very easy. Try it. You'll like it!

THE PAST, PRESENT, AND FUTURE SPREAD

This spread comes from the famed British Tarot author the late Richard Gardner, as presented in his book *The Tarot Speaks*. It is a shorter and quicker version of the Five-By-Five (Month-By-Month) Spread.

Starting at the left, lay down five cards in a row going from left to right. Above that row, going from left to right, lay down another five cards in a row. Do this for one other row. You now have three rows of cards with five cards in each row.

The bottom row represents the past or immediate past. The middle row is the present. The top row is the future or immediate future. The middle card for each row can be used as the focus of the issues affecting the querent, and you can apply the numerological personal months to these rows also.

THE *QUICK* PAST, PRESENT, AND FUTURE SPREAD

This is another variation of the Past, Present, and Future Spread that I developed. I call it the *Quick* Past, Present, and Future Spread. It can be used when you are in a big hurry. I frequently used this spread when working in Long Island discos, where speed was essential.

Starting at the left, lay down *three* cards in a row going from left to right. Above that row, going from left to right, lay down three cards. Do this for one other row. You now have three rows of only three cards each. The bottom row represents the past or immediate past. The middle row is the present. The top row is the future or immediate future. Incorporating the querent's numerological personal months (or personal days) this spread also adds to the effectiveness and speedy access of information.

THE THREE CARD SPREAD (*REAL QUICK PAST, PRESENT, AND FUTURE*)

This is a *real quick* past, present, and future. It is a *sophisticated version* of the E-Z Three Card Spread. Going from left to right, lay down three cards. The first card on the left indicates the past. The card in the middle represents the present and/or the querent. The card on the right stands for the future.

YES OR *NO* QUESTIONS (MY *PET PEEVES*)

I have already mentioned how difficult these questions are to answer. Firstly, remember the two prerequisites for the most taxing of all Tarot feats: a clear question and a calm mind. State the question clearly and in eight words or less. And meditate to calm your mind. Emotional anguish interferes with psychic reception.

For the most challenging of all divinations, I recommend the Horseshoe Spread and/or the Quick Yes or No. There are two methods of interpretation for each of these spreads. One is a *formula* technique; the other is an *interpretative* technique. The *interpretative* technique is very helpful for those occasional indirect responses; because even when the prerequisites are met, there are times when the cards refuse to yield a direct answer to the inquiry. (As we proceed, you shall see what I mean.)

For both techniques I have provided sample readings, and for each sample I shall pose the same exact query. It is the most commonly asked and the most difficult to answer. *Will he call?*

Comedian Jerry Seinfeld boils the answer down to a simple miscommunication between the genders. "When a woman says she'll call, she means *that day*, she'll call. When a man says he'll call, he means in his *lifetime*, he'll call."

Unfortunately the cards frequently reflect this vagueness. To add to the complication, this popular inquiry is usually accompanied by extremely high levels of *high anxiety*. This further emphasizes the importance of a tranquil psyche before attempting to tackle this most vexing of all questions.

THE HORSESHOE SPREAD

✳ THE FORMULA TECHNIQUE

This is based on a Yes or No Spread as presented by Lynn M. Buess in his book *The Tarot and Transformation*. I have added my personal flavor to this spread by putting it in the shape of a horseshoe. (The Horseshoe Spread is a Tarot standard with many variations to it.)

Formulate a clear question *before* shuffling is begun. *After* the question has been presented, the cards are shuffled and cut as usual. Or, instead of having the querent shuffle the cards, you can spread or fan them out in a straight line (facedown) and instruct the querent to pick seven cards, handing them to you one at a time as she goes along. Many people like this method because they feel involved in the selection of their *fates*.

Starting to the left, deal out (or place) seven cards while making the shape of a horseshoe (See Diagram 5.6).

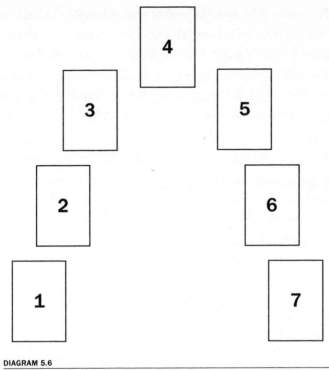

DIAGRAM 5.6

The Horseshoe Spread

In this spread the inverted cards play an important role. A card that is right-side-up is a *yes*. It is given a value of one point. An inverted card is a *no*. It is not given a value point. The *middle card* is given a value point of two if it is right-side-up; if inverted, no points. Quick addition of the value points of all seven cards gives an instant *yes* or *no* answer. Five to eight points is a *yes*. Three points or less is a *no*. Four points indicate there is no answer to the question at this time.

Let's look at some examples. Three cards are inverted; four cards are upright (including the two-point center card). That's five points. This is a *yes* answer.

Five cards are inverted. One card and the center card (two points) are right-side-up: three points. This is a *no* answer.

Now here is a brain twister. Three cards are inverted (including the two point middle card). The remaining four cards are right-side-up: four points. What's the answer? There isn't any. The cosmos has deemed this question to be unanswerable at this time.

✳ THE INTERPRETATIVE TECHNIQUE

Regardless of the answer given by the formula (point count) technique, you can still dig deeper for more information by interpreting the cards' positions. From left to right, the positions indicate: (1) the past; (2) the present; (3) the immediate future. The center or middle card (4) represents the querent and/or what the question is all about; (5) the attitude of another person; (6) an obstacle (if a positive card, this is reinforcing); and (7) the outcome.

This method is highly subjective, and the messages will not always be clear, cut-and-dry. Relate the cards to the question that is asked, and allow your *intuitive/psychic faculties* to factor into the interpretation.

Let's look at sample readings using both the *formula* and *interpretive* techniques for the eternal question: *Will he call?*

Felicia had met Anthony at a party ten days ago. He had promised to call but Felicia was growing doubtful. She wanted to know if there was any hope.

She clearly stated the question, *Will Anthony call?* She then shuffled and cut the deck. I dealt out seven cards following the Horseshoe Spread: The Sun, 4 of Pentacles (inverted),

Strength (inverted), 9 of Pentacles, 3 of Cups, Queen of Cups (inverted), and Knight of Cups. Pull the corresponding cards from your deck and follow along.

Starting with the *formula technique*, I calculated the points. Only three cards were inverted. The remaining cards, including the two-point center card, were right-side-up. This added up to five points, a *yes*. My prediction was that Anthony *would* call.

Using the *interpretative technique*, I could dig up more information. Follow along. Position 1—The Past, The Sun: Something recently past made Felicia happy and optimistic. She met Anthony. Position 2—The Present, 4 of Pentacles (inverted): She was trying to control her overexuberance. Position 3—The Immediate Future, Strength (inverted): She will be using all her will power to resist the urge to call *him*. Position 4—The Querent and/or What the Question Is All About, 9 of Pentacles: Felicia had been dressing up each day before going out, in case she ran into Anthony. Position 5—The Attitude of Another Person, 3 of Cups: I suggested Anthony liked to party. Position 6—An Obstacle, Queen of Cups (inverted): It looked as if Anthony could have had another lady on his mind. Position 7—The Outcome, Knight of Cups: This was the phone call from Anthony.

After the reading Felicia told me Anthony was known as a party animal; and, he had recently been jilted by a girl he really liked. However, two days later he called.

Here's another example. Gwen had been interested in a guy named Juan. He had asked for her number. But one month had passed, and Juan had not called. Distraught, she came to see me on the day of a full moon. She clearly stated the question, *Will he call?* Then I spread the cards out and instructed her to pick seven and hand them to me as she went along.

This is the order in which the cards were pulled: 7 of Swords, 8 of Swords (inverted), The Hanged Man, 9 of Swords (inverted), 7 of Cups (inverted), The Tower, and Knight of Wands (inverted). Arrange your cards accordingly and follow along.

Using the *formula* technique for the Horseshoe Spread, the interpretation was as follows. Four cards were inverted, including the two-point center card, leaving only three cards right-side-up. That totals to three, *a negative*. I informed Gwen that Juan would not call.

Gwen pressed me for details. I was able to accommodate her by using the *interpretative technique*.

Position 1—The Past, 7 of Swords: Something *sneaky* or deceptive had happened in the very recent past. Perhaps Juan had never really intended to call Gwen, but instead was leading her on. Position 2—The Present, 8 of Swords (inverted): Gwen was uncertain about what to do. I suggested she may have even felt this deception, but had been unable to admit it to herself. Position 3—The Immediate Future, The Hanged Man: Gwen would soon begin to feel taken advantage of. Position 4—The Querent and/or What the Question Is All About, 9 of Swords (inverted): Gwen was quite distressed over this situation. Position 5—The Attitude of Another Person, 7 of Cups (inverted): It appears as if Juan may, in fact, be an *untruthful* individual. Position 6—An Obstacle, The Tower: There would be an unexpected turn of events. Position 7—The Outcome, Knight of Wands (inverted): Although I firmly believed Juan would not call, he was still *in the picture*, but I could not be certain exactly how. And this is what I told Gwen, too.

Here's what happened. Two months passed and Juan never called. Gwen had completely forgotten about him. Then one

night at about eleven o'clock, she bumped into him in a conve-
nience store. He told her he had lost her phone number, and
asked for it again. Gwen fell for that *baloney* that's as old as the
hills and wrote it down for him. Of course, Juan never called
that time either, demonstrating that he was leading her on and
most likely made a habit out of practicing deception.

This is an excellent example of how life throws curve balls
that are reflected in the cards, but very difficult to discern.
While the direct answer to the question was not what Gwen
was looking for, there was a message coming through. Indeed,
the cards were telling something indirectly, but not specifically.
This is one of the most fascinating aspects of Tarot cards. Always *look at the cards*. It may only be in retrospect that the message becomes clear. This is why it is important to take dated
notes. In that way you will become more cognizant of how the
cards really talk.

Let's look at another sample. Kendra had had a huge argument with her boyfriend, Doug. They both said nasty and hurt-
ful things to each other. Kendra wondered if Doug would ever
call her again.

She clearly asked the question, shuffled, and cut. I dealt out
seven cards in the shape of a horseshoe. 5 of Swords (inverted),
3 of Swords (inverted), 2 of Swords, 7 of Wands, 5 of Cups, 10
of Swords (inverted), and Judgement (inverted). Set this
spread up with your cards and follow along.

Using the *formula* technique, four cards were inverted and
three cards were right-side-up (including the two point center
card). That was only a total of four points. In other words,
there was no answer at this time. Perhaps because the emotional investment in this question was too great; or perhaps it
was the universe's way of telling Kendra there was a spiritual

lesson to be learned from this experience and the outcome depended upon how she chose to respond to this situation. In other words, it was not simply a matter of Kendra *wanting* Doug to call her. Something else was going on here. Remember, the messages are always coming through, albeit cryptically.

Using the *interpretative* technique for this reading, I easily obtained more information. Without even looking at the cards' positions, a quick overview told me there was a lot of turmoil and stress. A breakdown was quite revealing. Position 1—The Past, 5 of Swords (inverted): There had recently been a bitter argument. Position 2—The Present, 3 of Swords (inverted): There was a lot of pain and anguish. Position 3—The Immediate Future, 2 of Swords: There was indecisiveness about what to do. Position 4—The Querent and/or What the Question Is All About, 7 of Wands: This card clued me in. It represented Kendra. She appeared to be quite controlling in this situation, and perhaps *control issues* were a part of *what the question was all about*. Position 5—The Attitude of Another Person, 5 of Cups: This definitely represented Doug. He felt quite wounded because of this *fierce fight*. Position 6—An Obstacle, 10 of Swords (inverted): I *sensed* this related again to Doug, who was also depressed. Position 7—The Outcome, Judgement (inverted): This looked like a phone call, but not *from* Doug. Instead it looked as if Kendra would call him.

At this point I paused, because I *got the picture*. I had an intuitive flash. It appeared to me as if Kendra had initiated this brutal battle. Because of her controlling nature (7 of Wands), she refused to accept responsibility for a situation she herself had created and wanted Doug to call her. That is, she wanted to *make* Doug call her. However she should have been calling Doug to apologize. But, I did not want to put ideas into her head by suggesting this. I wanted her to come to this realization for herself.

During the brief intermission of my pause, Kendra began talking. She admitted to having deliberately pressed Doug's buttons just to get a reaction out of him; only she hadn't realized how badly she was really hurting him. Since I had said he was not going to call her, she quietly asked me if she should call him to apologize. I advised her that I thought the last card, Judgement, was saying just that.

For Kendra, this was a lesson in personal growth. She learned that for everything you do in life there is a price to be paid. And responsibility must be taken for our actions. It was the Tarot cards that aided in vividly bringing this irrevocable cosmic law to her awareness.

A QUICK *YES* OR *NO*

✳ THE FORMULA TECHNIQUE

This spread is from *Mastering the Tarot* by Eden Gray. Pose the question clearly before anything else is begun. The cards are then shuffled and cut as usual or fanned out to be selected by the querent. Deal out three cards or ask the querent to pick three cards, handing them to you in the order in which they are pulled. Lay them out side-by-side, going left to right. The answer is determined by how many cards are right-side-up or inverted. All three cards right-side-up, a definite *yes*. Three cards inverted, a definite *no*. Two cards right-side-up, a *qualified yes*. Two cards inverted, a *qualified no*. *Qualified*, in this case, means there are modifying influences affecting the matter, such as restrictions. Or, perhaps the matter is subject to certain conditions being met before it can effectively transpire. I told you, life is not always clear, cut-and-dry!

✷ THE INTERPRETATIVE TECHNIQUE

By reading (*feeling*) the three cards that come up in this spread and relating them to the question that is being asked, they can be interpreted in the context of the query. You can even weave the Three Card Spread (*Real Quick* Past, Present, and Future) into the *interpretative* technique for extra information. Use your *intuitive/psychic faculties* freely with this spread. You will be amazed at the insights you'll have!

Let's look at sample readings for this spread using both the *formula* and *interpretive* techniques for that eternal question: *Will he call?*

Jennifer had met Russ a few days ago. Russ was a star athlete, in med school, and quite handsome. Jennifer was chewing her fingernails to the quick wondering if Russ would get in touch with her. She asked the question, *Will Russ call?* I spread the deck out, facedown. She picked three cards and handed them to me as she went along. I placed them down, going from left to right.

The 2 of Cups, Ace of Cups and 7 of Pentacles were all right-side-up. I told Jennifer, Russ would definitely call.

By looking at the individual cards, more information could be obtained. The 2 of Cups definitely meant a relationship. Love was in the air! The Ace of Cups suggests happy emotions and the predominating suit of Cups told me that something was going to happen soon, maybe in one day or one week. But the 7 of Pentacles said that something would also be around for a very long time. Seeds were being planted. There was more going on here than just a phone call. I told this to Jennifer.

Let's incorporate the Three Card Spread (*Real Quick* Past, Present, and Future) into this interpretation. The 2 of Cups, the immediate past—a relationship appeared to be blooming. Ace of Cups, the immediate present, indicated a phone message is currently waiting. This middle card can also be interpreted as the querent. Jennifer is happy and optimistic. The 7 of Pentacles, the immediate future, suggested that the seeds for a long-term situation were being planted.

When Jennifer got back to her room, his message awaited her. They went together for several years, then married. Russ wanted to get through med school first. They are still a very happy couple!

Here's another example. Grace wanted to know if Phil would call. Phil was a charismatic guy, who attended a college about one-and-a-half hours away from Grace. A friend had tried to fix them up, and gave Phil Grace's number.

Grace clearly asked the question. I spread the cards out face-down. She picked three and handed them to me as she went along. Going from left to right, I placed them down. The 6 of Swords, Temperance, and The Lovers were all inverted. I advised Grace that Phil would definitely not call.

I was still able to get more information for Grace by looking at the overall picture(s). In this instance I was working totally on intuition. Focusing on the cards, I didn't like what I saw. Based on the feeling I was getting, Phil appeared to be unstable in relationships. Grace confided that he was reputed to go from one girlfriend to the next. I told Grace she should be glad she would never hear from him. However, The Lovers did come up in the spread, although inverted. I *felt* as if it was signaling an important message. There may be another opportunity. Grace informed me that another guy had indeed been asking her out. But she had been putting him off, hoping that Phil would call. After the reading, Grace decided to forget about Phil and accept a date with the other prospect. This is yet another example of how the direct message may be unfavorable but an indirect message is coming through, which is significant.

Adding the Three Card Spread to the interpretation, there is more information that can be drawn. Remember, *all* the cards are inverted. The 6 of Swords, the immediate past: Phil was not near Grace, but at some distance attending another college. Temperance, the present: A situation that was not going to change. As the querent, Grace was *trying to balance for time*. Keep in mind, I'm *feeling* here and in *intuitive/psychic* mode. The Lovers, the future, showed that there was indeed another guy calling.

Let's look at another example. Keisha and Dwayne dated on and off for a while. Then they drifted apart. It had been more than six months since Keisha had seen him.

Keisha formulated the question, *Will Dwayne call?* I spread the cards out face down. Keisha picked three cards and handed them to me one by one: the 6 of Pentacles, King of Cups and the 7 of Wands (inverted). One card was inverted, the other two were right-side-up. The answer was a *qualified* yes. That meant Dwayne probably would call if certain conditions were met. Or, the call was subject to restrictions. But, that was vague. I had to dig deeper to give Keisha more information; and, here, again, my intuition was going to be the guide.

The 6 of Pentacles said that maybe Dwayne had had to borrow money. If he was having financial problems, he may not have felt good about himself and uncomfortable about talking to Keisha at this time. This was basic psychology. I saw Dwayne as the King of Cups, a man floating on the ocean. Perhaps Dwayne was drifting along in life, going wherever the tide was taking him. The 7 of Wands (inverted) looked like a message. But Wands could have meant months down the road. So I told Keisha that if Dwayne gets himself together and plants his feet on the ground, she would hear from him within a few months.

These cards fit easily into the Three Card Spread. The 6 of Pentacles, the past: Dwayne had to borrow money. The King of Cups, the present: Dwayne is presently floating aimlessly. This position can also be interpreted as the querent. Dwayne is strongly on Keisha's mind. The 7 of Wands (inverted), the future, indicated there will be a message.

Five months later he sent her a letter, *snail-mail*. While this was not a phone call, it was nevertheless a communication. But, maybe not exactly what Keisha had in mind. And, remember, I said it was *qualified*. This is another example of how things play out much differently than our *imagined* expectations.

Here is another example. Alex, who was quite a charmer, had been flirting around with Rachel and had asked for her number. One month had passed and she had not heard from him.

Rachel asked the question, *Will Alex call?* She picked three cards and handed them to me one by one: the 6 of Cups, the Ace of Swords (inverted), and the Page of Wands (inverted). One card was right-side-up; the other two were inverted. The answer was a *qualified* no. But what did that mean?

I dug deeper and looked at the individual cards. It certainly looked like a message to me. I told Rachel the only perception

I could get was that he most likely would not call her, but I did see something about a message or phone call. I had no idea what that meant. This, however, was what my intuition was telling me.

Using a quick analysis of the Three Card Spread, the cards did not fit so neatly. Nevertheless, something could be seen. The 6 of Cups, the past: Rachel had given Alex her number. The Ace of Swords (inverted), the present and the querent: Rachel was anxious about a message. The Page of Wands (inverted), the future: There would be a phone call.

About two weeks passed. One day the phone rang. Rachel answered it. A man's voice asked to speak to Patricia, Rachel's gorgeous roommate. It was Alex!

Indeed there was a phone call but not the one Rachel had hoped for. This is an excellent example of how the universe throws us curve balls which are many times impossible to adroitly *catch*.

I must reemphasize that you will have to experiment with these spreads to see what works for you. Always interpret the cards in the context of the question being asked. Since you are working in *intuitive/psychic* mode, everything may not fit exactly. This is Tarot card reading, not mathematics!

If you are uncertain about the message trying to come through, it's okay to say so. But always remember to *look at the cards and say what you see*.

WILMA CARROLL'S PARTY SPREAD

Here is an extra added bonus. This is a spread I developed myself (See Diagram 5.7). In fact, as *you* become more comfort-

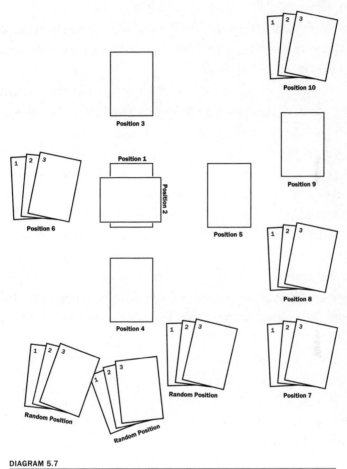

Position 3

Position 10

Position 1

Position 2

Position 6

Position 9

Position 5

Position 8

Position 4

Position 7

Random Position

Random Position

Random Position

DIAGRAM 5.7

Wilma Carroll's Party Spread

able with the cards, you may also find yourself *guided* to develop your own spread. You may find yourself, one day, unconsciously laying the cards out in a virtually unique spread of your very own creation. Many Tarot card readers do this.

This one came to me quite naturally. It was the result of reading at hundreds of parties, special events, and colleges—where time is of the essence.

Start with the *Advanced* Celtic Cross Spread. After reading the cards in that spread, without picking them up, continue with a quick and short variation of the Seven Sisters Spread. Deal the next three cards from the top of the unused deck and throw them (in that group of three) anywhere on top of the Advanced Celtic Cross Spread or *randomly* around the spread. There is no formal positioning with these extra cards. Read that group of three cards as you would in the Seven Sisters Spread. Continue this *random throw* two or three times, or even four times more, as long as you feel you have an intuitive connection. If you are getting nothing from the group of three cards, try using only two cards. Experiment and see what works for you.

THE ULTIMATE QUESTION

"Do You Ever Get Any Great Revelations?"

"You're all *wrong!*" he snapped.

"No dear. She's *right!*" his wife shot back. "You're very accurate!" She turned to me.

"I don't believe in this stuff!" he growled. Gerald was a retired high-ranking naval officer. I was reading at his nephew's bar mitzvah. I sat there and kept my mouth shut as husband and wife slugged it out. I had witnessed this scene many times before. Men disagree with me, no matter how accurate I am, while their wives confirm everything I am saying! In fact when I first started reading at parties, I wouldn't read for a man unless his wife was sitting there with him. Now, with nearly four decades of experience under my belt, I am better prepared to handle this situation. This is also aided by the somewhat changing New Millennium mentality. In other words, men are not quite as skeptical. But they are *still* not true believers.

"All right," mumbled Gerald, "you're accurate."

He *was* impressed. The Tarot cards had correctly described an important upcoming meeting and the costly repair work being done in his kitchen. In typical male style, however, he remained adamantly unyielding in his skepticism.

"You still haven't convinced me there's anything to this."

Gerald glared at me for several seconds, then slowly leveled a sly look. A devilish grin spread across his face. I braced myself for what was coming. I knew exactly what he was going to say.

"Do you ever get any *great* revelations?" he snickered with a *tongue-in-cheek* attitude.

Gerald could not resist asking what I call *the ultimate question.* It is occasionally asked by men, but *always* accompanied with a noticeably facetious undertone. Yet it is a question for which I have a very serious answer. Yes! Absolutely! I can honestly tell you that during my thirty-seven years of experience with Tarot cards, I have had many great, fascinating, and unbelievable *revelations*!

In this anecdotal chapter I recount the details of many of these incredible experiences. And it is deliberately placed near the end of the book, as I did not want anyone to be influenced by *my* particular style of interpretation. So when I tell you which cards came up in a particular reading, keep in mind, this is *my* way of seeing things and definitely not the only way to see things. Certainly by now you have had some of your own profound revelations with Tarot cards.

Because these stories span a period of more than three decades, I am not able to remember *all* the cards that appeared in each spread. But, I do remember (in most instances) at least three or four, and that should give you an idea of how I came to these well-founded conclusions.

* * *

Picture this! It was my *second* professional reading. Amanda, an attractive redhead, was a referral from my *first* professional client. I vividly remembered Amanda from junior high school. Popular and well liked by everyone, she had been known for her wry sense of humor. My friends and I used to tell her she would make a great stand-up comic, but unfortunately that was not the route she had taken. Rushing into marriage right after high school, she was now left to raise two children on her own. Her ex-husband was nowhere to be found and, of course, neither were the child support payments. So Amanda worked full time as a salesperson in a department store.

As we sat in my study on a freezing February evening, sipping hot tea to keep us warm, I began doing the Five-By-Five (Month-By-Month) Spread. In the row representing *the present* was The Empress, right smack in the middle. I knew the focus was a mother. I do not remember the surrounding cards, but in the row above were many Major Trump cards: The Star, Temperance, The Moon, and Judgement. That meant events were imminent. When I began reading this spread, my mind went blank. Amanda later told me that I put my hand over the cards and sat there *hemming and hawing* for about five minutes.

Finally I said, "When the time comes to let your mother go, do so knowing she will always be with you in spirit and guiding you."

I had no idea why I was saying this. It didn't make any sense to me, but my intuition was telling me something and the words seemed to fall from my mouth. Amanda then told me her mother was dying of cancer. She was not expected to live more than three days. Chills ran up and down my spine. Three days later her mother passed away.

What a way to start a career! Leading off with the most sensitive, serious, and taboo issue of all! Months later Amanda told me the reading had comforted her, and she could actually feel her mother's presence *in spirit*, guiding her as she reared her children.

But this was not at all comforting to me. I went on to see *death* in the cards two more times!

The second time occurred when I was reading at a discotheque on Long Island. I was still new as a professional reader, only six months into my career. The manager and the owner of the club sat down for readings. Bob, the manager, was no stranger to psychic readings. He had been a regular client of Long Island's famous Egg Lady, a Scottish woman, renowned for her phenomenal readings using *eggs*!

The Egg Lady had died about one-and-a-half years before I moved to Long Island, so I never had the privilege of meeting her. But I learned all about her from her clients, many of whom I inherited. They all regaled me with stories of her amazing clairvoyance and eccentric behavior.

Mrs. D. lived in a comfortable house in Suffolk County, located in the middle of Long Island. She had come to the United States after marrying an American serviceman she had met during World War II. He died years earlier, and she fully earned her living (and a decent one at that) reading eggs.

Getting an appointment with her was no easy task, the wait sometimes being a good six months! People would drive several hours from as far away as Pennsylvania to see her, and as soon as she was tired, she would stop.

"It didn't matter how long you had been waiting or how far you had driven. If there was a long line of cars waiting outside her house, it didn't matter. She would run out into the street and scream that she was tired and had to stop. You would have to reschedule!" a former client told me.

Mrs. D. would crack an egg into a cup and then stir it with her finger. She would then look at the egg and ask, "Do you want to hear everything?" If you said, "yes," she would tell you *all*, even about serious illness and approaching death.

One time Mrs. D. told a man his wife would have an affair. And she did. He was so angered he returned to the Egg Lady and beat her up. (So you see, I'm not the only one to have difficulties reading for men. Fortunately, my experiences have not been that severe.) After that she refused to read for *any* man but ultimately agreed to accept five gentlemen whom she deemed were *special*. Eventually I read for three of the *chosen few*.

As I commenced the reading with Bob, I remember thinking that the Egg Lady was a tough act to follow. Yet despite my inexperience, my performance was to get rave reviews, although somewhat delayed.

I went on to tell Bob about another business he had, a travel agency. I also mentioned some real estate deals in which he was involved. In the position of the *home*, using the Advanced Celtic Cross Spread, I saw the 9 of Swords, the 6 of Swords, and the Queen of Wands. That is all I remember.

My prediction was as follows: "A woman will be leaving your life, someone close to you like a sister." Again I had no idea what this meant. It was a strangely cryptic statement, but once again the words sort of fell out of my mouth. My intuition was guiding me.

At the end of the reading Bob looked at the owner of the club, who had been listening intently. "Interesting, isn't it?" commented Bob. They both exchanged nods. It wasn't until two years later that the story unraveled.

Meanwhile I had moved into Manhattan and lost touch with the people at the disco. By a strange twist of fate I was invited back to read on a Saturday night in June. The club now had new owners, but Bob remained as the manager. He greeted me warmly at the door and I inquired about his wife. I had spoken to her and his sister a couple of times on the phone. They had been thinking of booking appointments with me for private consultations but we never could coordinate the times.

"My wife died," he said.

"I'm so sorry!" I gasped. I was stunned and very concerned and continued extending my condolences. "What happened?"

"She died of a congenital heart disease. *You* predicted it."

Instantly I went on the defensive. "I *never* predict death!" I screamed in a panicky voice. "It would be unethical."

He then reminded me of the reading when I told him a woman would be leaving his life. His wife had been ill for a long time, and they both knew she did not have long to live. My cryptic message made sense. And in spite of my policy of never predicting death, the cards had their own unique way of conveying the message *symbolically*. This was the second time I had inadvertently predicted death.

With the first two predictions the querents both knew that someone close to them would soon die. I was reading, or pulling, this information directly from their conscious minds. However, the third time I saw death in the cards the reading was more dramatic. This time I pulled the information from the querent's subconscious mind. She had no idea that someone close to her was about to die.

A pleasant woman with graying hair sat before me as I did the Advanced Celtic Cross Spread followed by the Advanced Horoscope Spread. Beverly had been referred to me by her neighbor, who was a regular client.

"I've always been curious about this," she told me. "But I never got around to doing it."

I was going around the houses in the Advanced Horoscope Spread when I stopped at the Ninth House. I read the cards: Justice, Ace of Pentacles, and 10 of Pentacles. I told Beverly she and her husband would be talking to a lawyer and/or an accountant about real estate matters. This was consistent with what appeared to be the entire theme of the reading. Beverly and her husband would come into some money, sell their home and buy a new one some distance away. Beverly kept insisting that she could not relate to a thing I was saying. I kept insisting she take notes because it would all make sense sooner or later. (This is a good example of how you must always trust what you see in the cards, even if the querent disagrees. When you project into the future many times people cannot relate to what you are saying because it seems so remote or impossible. The querent may start arguing with you. Do not get into an argument. But stick to what you see in the cards!)

Suddenly I realized I had accidentally skipped over the Eighth House. (It was really not an accident. *Nothing ever happens by accident*, according to occultists. But, on a subconscious level I must have known something was up.) I didn't want Beverly to think I was careless so I didn't say anything. Instead, I quietly backtracked to the Eighth House and picked

up the cards. (The Eighth House deals with taxes, inheritances, other people's money, insurance, sex, and death or
manner of death. It is the most difficult to understand of all
the houses in the horoscope because it deals with transformation.) The Empress was surrounded by Death and the 10 of
Swords. Some Tarot experts think the 10 of Swords is the
worst card in the deck. And, as I have said in Chapter 3
the Death card does not mean physical death. When it falls in
the Eighth House, however, its significance may have to be
reconsidered.

"Is your mother still alive?" I asked.

"Oh, no!" she said. "My mother died years ago."

What I never thought to ask was, "Is your *mother-in-law* still
alive?" Two days later Beverly's mother-in-law died suddenly of
a stroke. She was in her late eighties and in good health. Her
death came as a shock to everyone. Her house had been willed
to Beverly and her husband. They sold it, plus their own house,
and bought a much nicer one far away. Of course they had to
talk to a lawyer and an accountant. This was one of the most
incredible experiences I have ever had with Tarot cards.

Not all of my readings have been so dramatic. I have had
light, pleasant, and even funny experiences with the Tarot.
Annette, for instance. When she came to me for a reading I saw
The Sun, The Empress, and the 6 of Cups in the position representing *you* in the Advanced Celtic Cross Spread. I predicted
a baby being born, but since she looked about eighteen years of
age and much too young to be having a baby, I thought it might
be a sister who would have the baby and Annette would be the
one caring for it. Annette blushed a deep red and then confided
that she had come for the reading to see if *she* was pregnant.
Twenty-eight years old (a young looking twenty-eight), mar-

ried and as *pretty as a picture;* she was impatiently awaiting the results of the pregnancy test. In those days it took two weeks to get the results. Home testing kits had not yet been developed. I told her I definitely saw a baby being born. Two weeks later, four of her friends came in for readings and confirmed the test was positive!

When Jocelyn came to me for a reading I saw The Empress, The Sun, and the Queen of Cups, all indications of a pregnancy. Since this was the first consultation I had ever had with her, and didn't know her at all, I gently eased into what I viewed as a potentially sensitive issue. I did not want to blurt out, "I think you're pregnant!" As it turned out, Elizabeth, a successful interior designer with her own business, already had a little girl and wanted to have another child eventually but didn't know when.

"I think you're pregnant now," I informed her.

She immediately purchased a home pregnancy test and returned a few weeks later with the good news. She *was* pregnant!

"And it's a good thing you told me," she laughed. "I was getting ready to go on vacation and eat, drink, and be merry!" A year later she returned with her darling baby boy!

Working with the Advanced Horoscope Spread, I was reading for Sasha, a stylish and elegant young woman from Brooklyn. In the first house was the Queen of Cups, 9 of Pentacles, and Queen of Wands.

"You're surrounded by women," I told her. "You do something to make them beautiful. Are you in the cosmetics business?"

"I own a hair salon," she told me.

The 7 of Wands, 5 of Swords and Justice fell in the Ninth House. In the Tenth House was the 10 of Wands, 9 of Swords, and 5 of Pentacles. In the Seventh House was the Knight of Swords, 8 of Wands, and 6 of Wands.

This looked like a power struggle with a judge or a lawyer over a legal matter that would have an affect on her business. There was also a lot of paperwork or papers to be signed. Sasha had no idea what I was talking about. She insisted she was not involved in any legal dispute and had no reason to talk to an attorney. But the cards were clear. I was telling it exactly as I saw it! If there were no legal issues at that moment, they were certain to come up soon.

A few weeks later Sasha phoned. She had been called up for jury duty! She was expected to serve for two weeks.

"But I run my own business!" she screamed. "I can't be gone for two weeks."

Sasha had already gone before a judge and asked to be permanently excused from this most inconvenient civil service. They had a heated argument and power struggle. The judge insisted she had no chance whatsoever of getting out of jury duty. She had hired a lawyer to help her. And, while frantically worrying about her business, there were a lot of letters (paperwork) going back and forth.

I reminded her of the reading and my prediction. This was exactly what I had seen in the cards. Sasha remembered what I had said; but, nevertheless there was another complication. She had taped the session. The tape recorder had worked perfectly when we began. However when she went home and tried to replay it, all she heard was a blurred noise.

Meanwhile, Sasha wanted to know what the outcome would be. This is one of the toughest challenges with any form of divination. Trying to intercept the *Universal Mind* can be a frustrating task. Astrologers defend this perplexity by explaining that it is easy to see that there will be rough road ahead, but, how a situation will actually conclude—and in whose favor—is impossible many times to determine. I have staunchly disagreed with my colleagues on this because I think by digging deeper, you can get some idea which way the tide will turn. Perhaps not all the specifics but many indications of the aftermath or the conditions following the *rocky road* can definitely be ascertained.

I remembered initially telling Sasha there would be a favorable outcome to a legal matter. Since this was a spontaneous response, uninfluenced by any *concrete* knowledge of a legal matter, it was an accurate psychic insight. The cards had also told of a lot of aggravation and stress before this matter was settled. According to Sasha, that part of the prediction was already occurring. I felt confident in assuring her she would be granted a lengthy postponement. And, she was. She called me several weeks later to tell me, with relief, she had been given a year-and-a-half deferment.

Since the querent had no idea that a notice for jury duty was coming, this was a genuine psychic projection and an excellent example of how strong psychic energy can interfere with mechanical equipment.

It was early in my career, about one year, when I learned a cardinal rule about reading Tarot cards. You never know what you'll see when you look into someone's cards. *Things aren't always what they seem to be.*

It was picture perfect: Mommy, Daddy and a nine-month-old baby son. They looked like the most ordinary up-and-coming middle class family out for a Friday evening dinner. I was reading in a Long Island restaurant when the charming couple invited me over to their table to read for *Daddy.*

The Tower, Justice, 8 of Swords, 3 of Swords, and 5 of Pentacles fell in the spread. I spoke of *restrictions*, serious legal and financial problems. I was interpreting the symbols and not able to directly relate them to any specific situation. This frequently happens when you are trying to interpret something that is not even in your framework of thinking. Therefore I had no idea what I was saying when I spoke about *restrictions*, although it certainly did not look good.

After the reading, Daddy, who appeared to be the perfect husband and father, unabashedly told me he was in *big* trouble for *embezzling* and was facing a possible three years' imprisonment! Fortunately the outcome did not look so grim. I advised him he might have to pay a hefty fine and be able to get out of prison time.

Shocked and shaken by this unwholesome predicament, I remained tactful, non-judgmental, and maintained a professional demeanor. Then I made a quick *exit stage left*.

You will see a lot of things when reading Tarot cards. Get ready!

Now this is a story of how I used my knowledge of astrology and numerology combined with Tarot cards to come up with a *not-so-welcome* insight. One icy January weekend I was working at a birthday party in Hoboken, New Jersey. Amy was an entrepreneurial young woman who worked in sales, earning quite a substantial living. Her friends were delightful, and even the men were enjoying my readings until the football game started. At that point, they all gathered around the television in the living room, leaving the women and me alone in the large dining room. Amy was the last to have a reading. She had waited until all of her guests had had a turn.

Doing the Advanced Celtic Cross Spread, at the top, in the

position of *culmination*, I saw The Lovers and The High Priestess. It was three days before a full moon. Secrets come out on the full moon. Amy was also in a 7 personal year. Any relationship started in that year usually has a serious obstacle, another person. I find many women in a 7 personal year will unknowingly or knowingly get involved with a married man. If it is unknowing, imagine the jarring reality check when I tell them. Such was the case with Amy. She had told me she had just started seeing this man.

"I think he is also seeing someone else," I gently told her.

"No, he's not!" she snapped at me defensively.

I stuck to my guns. The Lovers next to The High Priestess were enough confirmation for me. The High Priestess was the secret. Next to The Lovers, it meant a secret love or secret about love. Three days before the full moon and Amy's 7 personal year told me my prediction was an indisputable fact.

Amy called me two weeks later.

"He *was* seeing someone else! That blankity, blankity, S.O.B.! Blah! Blah! Blah!" Amy was furious.

Then she turned her anger on me.

"How did you know? How did you know?"

"I'm a psychic," I calmly stated. "That's my job."

This is what I mean about *venting*. It is very draining on a psychic when a client does this. *Being a psychic is a thankless job.* . . .

Here is another example of how I used my knowledge of astrology and numerology with Tarot cards to make an interesting prediction. I was using the Advanced Celtic Cross Spread, as a woman inquired about her boyfriend. She had not seen him for quite a while. The Magician, The Hierophant, the 4 of Wands, the 6 of Cups, the 3 of Pentacles, and the Knight of Wands appeared in the spread. I told her he was in New Jersey (the Knight of Wands faced left, pointing west of New York, which is New Jersey) with religious people (The Hierophant), who were also his friends (6 of Cups). They were helping him get things under control (The Magician). Numerologically, she was in a 5 personal day which brings *unexpected* happenings. Astrologically, Venus was going retrograde, which brings *old loves* back on the scene. (This is advanced astrology but something you will naturally absorb by osmosis. Another planetary phenomenon known as Mercury retrograde is a term becoming very mainstream nowadays. This you will also pick-up via osmosis.) I added that she might hear from him that evening. She then informed me that he had a drinking problem, and she thought he had gone to a monastery in New Jersey where the monks were kind to him and would help him to deal with his alcoholism.

That evening he showed up at the restaurant where she worked. He had, in fact, been with the monks in New Jersey.

I was working at a fortieth birthday party in Forest Hills, New York. It is a magnificent neighborhood with stately old homes, and the party actually took place in a large Victorian house.

I had read for the hostess, Jaclyn, who was also the *birthday girl*. The last person to be read was her husband, Martin. They were a lovely couple, each with their own thriving businesses, and they had two young sons.

Martin shuffled the cards. I dealt out the Advanced Celtic Cross Spread.

"It's so *confusing!*" I gulped. "There is so much disorganization." I couldn't make any sense out of it. None of the cards connected with each other and with my experience, I should have been able to have seen something in this spread.

Jaclyn burst out laughing, "Martin is disorganized. You got it!" This is a good example of how you literally have to say what you see. My instant impression was that of *disorganization*. And it actually played directly into a correct interpretation.

I asked Martin to reshuffle the cards, while noting he was in a 5 personal year. This means *expect the unexpected*. Viewing the new spread, in the position of the *home*, was the 4 of Wands, 10 of Cups, and the 10 of Pentacles. In the position representing the querent (*you*) was The Tower. In September Martin would be in a 5 personal month as well as a 5 personal year, a double whammy of *expect the unexpected*.

"You're going to move in September," I informed him.

"But we just moved into this house a few months ago!" shrieked the *birthday girl*. "I don't want to move again!"

Once more, I stuck to my guns while husband and wife kept insisting they would not be moving in the near future. Several months later, Jaclyn called to invite me to work at their son's bar mitzvah.

"I must tell you this," Jaclyn's voice bubbled with enthusiasm. "In September, Martin suddenly decided he couldn't stand that house; so we moved to another only a few blocks away. We were really impressed with your prediction; although we both disagreed, you didn't waver at all."

The moral of this story is, always call it as you see it.

One time I was reading at a corporate Christmas party. I told one of the hostesses she would have a problem with her car. The Knight of Swords fell next to the Knight of Pentacles. After the party she went to her car which was parked on the street. It had a big dent in it!

Interestingly enough, car problems are fairly easy to pick up on. The Knight of Swords falling near The Chariot (symbolizing a vehicle) or another knight is a sure indication of this. Case in point, the reading I gave a student at a small midwestern college.

I had been imported to a small college in a small town (outside of Omaha, Nebraska) with a population of only seven thousand. In that neck of the woods, the students had never seen anything like a real-life *fortune-teller*, and the advisor wanted to expose them to many aspects of the *real world*. It was a very receptive crowd.

One student in particular caught my eye. He was an older student with a fascinating multicolored necktie. I gave him a very upbeat forecast, except for my closing statement. The Knight of Swords fell next to The Chariot.

"You are going to have trouble with a car," I affirmed.

A few weeks later, I received a thoughtful letter from the student. He complimented me on the accurate reading and said I had converted him to a true believer. However, he had been certain that my forecast about a car problem would never come to pass because he had recently purchased a brand-new Saturn, well-known for reliability. That afternoon he was driving on the highway towards Omaha when a car from behind plowed into him. He knew instantly that was the car problem. I wrote back expressing my sorrow about the car and thanking him for being so gracious as to give me the much appreciated feedback.

Another time I told a client she would take an unexpected trip and meet a lawyer who would become her friend and business partner. Justice, The World, and the 2 of Cups fell in the Ninth House of the Advanced Horoscope Spread. The Tower was in the Third House. A few days later she made an unexpected visit to Philadelphia and met a lawyer who soon became her business advisor and friend.

Using the Advanced Horoscope Spread for a querent, the 5 of Swords, the Queen of Wands, and the Ace of Wands came up in the Eighth House. This looked like a difficulty with an insurance matter but it would be resolved. A few days later my client got into a squabble about an insurance matter (5 of Swords in the Eighth House of other people's money). A pleasant, fair-minded woman (Queen of Wands) sided with my client. Within one month (Ace of Wands) payment of the money due was received.

While attending a college conference one October, I gave a reading to a coed from an exclusive school near Philadelphia. The Knight of Swords, King of Swords, Ace of Swords, The Magician, and the Queen of Wands came up in the spread. I told her she would have a problem with a car and an authority figure, a cryptic message. However, here again I was reading the symbols.

Months later the committee brought me in for the Spring Fling. The student couldn't wait to tell me what had happened. It was early one evening when her boss, the student activities director, asked her to run an errand for the committee.

"She told me to take her car," said the coed. "Then I accidentally parked in a no-parking zone. I hadn't realized it. I just parked and ran the errand. When I returned to the car, a cop was standing there writing a ticket. I got into a big fight with him. You also told me I had a bad temper. Then the cop wanted to see the car registration. When he saw it wasn't my car, he thought I'd stolen it. I told him I had permission to use it. But he didn't believe me and called my boss. What a mess!"

It was a Tuesday evening. I had just given myself a manicure when the phone rang. Gingerly I picked up the receiver so as not to smudge the wet fingernails. It was a friend calling. She wanted to refer a woman from out of town to me.

"She wants to talk to a psychic," my friend told me. "Can you see her right away?"

"Yes," I said. But I secretly worried about ruining my perfect manicure.

It was a needless concern because by the time the referral and her husband arrived at my apartment, my nails were dry and I was able to work dexterously with the cards. They were a stunning couple. A beautiful Southern belle and handsome husband, both chicly dressed; they made Barbie and Ken look plain.

I commenced with the reading, starting with the Advanced Celtic Cross Spread. The first card that came up was The Moon.

"Your dreams are telling you something," I reported.

The woman immediately told me she had been having a recurring dream that disturbed her. That's why she wanted the consultation.

This is an excellent example of *instant focus*. I had immediately locked into psychic mode and made a connection with the first card that was placed down. I had threaded the needle! And, the recurring dream was the whole key to the reading.

Still, I continued laying out the cards. The Queen of Swords, 7 of Cups, 7 of Swords, and 9 of Wands came up. I suggested there was lot of jealousy around her from other women. It was not surprising because the lady was so gorgeous! She was aware of problems with three women in her office. She was also in the position to terminate them and thought that was exactly what she would have to do. But it was the validation of the frequent dream in the Tarot card, The Moon, that gave the lovely lady the most reassuring insight and the strength to trust the messages from her own subconscious mind.

December 13, 1994. *TV Tokyo* was interviewing psychics in various international cities for a variety show. I was the *designated hitter* for The Big Apple, New York City, the greatest city in the world!

Several Japanese technicians swarmed about my midsize New York City studio apartment. Speaking in Japanese, which is *not* my second language, they swiftly ran around pulling out plugs, hooking up lights, and literally taking over my humble dwelling.

"You unplugged the VCR!" I gasped. I had wanted to catch them before they pulled out *that* plug. VCRs are so complicated to program. But it was too late.

To further add to the confusion, the young Japanese reporter hardly spoke English. When it was lights, camera, action, he asked me in a thick accent, "What do you see for Japan?"

I had never before been asked to give a reading for a country. I was curious about what the cards would say. I spread them out on my desk facedown. "Pick three," I instructed him.

One-by-one, he handed me three cards, The World, The Tower and the 10 of Swords. The message was clear and terrifying.

"An earthquake," I whispered. "I see an earthquake."

January 17, 1995. A devastating earthquake hit the populous Japanese city of Kobe. The cards had predicted it. This was one of the most unusual revelations I had ever seen them yield. It clearly illustrates their unfathomable power.

For the record, this interview never aired in the United

States but only in Japan on December 17, 1994. The prophecy was edited out. Television is entertainment and negative forecasts are unwelcome. Instead I was featured answering questions about Michael Jackson. I did however call the producer and the reporter, who both remembered the extraordinary augury.

It can only get worse. December 2000. This uncanny revelation will haunt me forever. For the third year in a row, I was invited to entertain at an exclusive corporate Christmas party. As we sailed around New York Harbor on a luxurious yacht, I nonchalantly helped myself to the caviar and scrumptious hors d'oeuvres.

A woman I remembered from the previous years sat before me and shuffled the cards. The Tower, the 4 of Wands, and the 10 of Pentacles came up in the spread. At that time she was in a 4 personal year. But in 2001 she would be in a 5 personal year, and in September of 2001 she would be in a 5 personal month, a *double dose* of *expect the unexpected*! The 4 of Wands and the 10 of Pentacles looked like an office to me. With The Tower next to it and the numerological vibration of the *unpredictable* coming up, I predicted there would be a *new* office in September of 2001.

"There are no plans for a new office," she countered

"Maybe the company will be growing rapidly," I insisted.

She shook her head. "No, no."

We were seated on a plush white, horseshoe-shaped leather couch, and surrounded by several other people. They all knew me well enough to agree that when Wilma says it's going to happen, it's going to happen. But everyone listening firmly disagreed with my forecast and maintained another office was a total improbability. However, I saw the same indication for two other people, The Tower appearing in both of their spreads.

September 11, 2001. Their office was on the eighty-ninth floor of Tower One! Thank God they all got out safely! Quickly they moved to a new office in another part of Manhattan.

One of the most astonishing episodes of my Tarot card adventures took place on live television. It was October 31, 2000, *Halloween*. I was invited to appear on *Live With Regis*. What an honor! What an opportunity!

The show was momentarily in a state of flux. Kathie Lee had just left, and Regis was still looking for another co-host. Each day they had a different pinch hitter and on this particular Halloween, Regis was joined by his stunning wife, Joy. The set was decorated like a medieval castle and Regis and Joy were dressed as a medieval king and queen. Wardrobe wrapped me in a purple velvet cape with a high collar, so I would have a wizardly look.

Regis Philbin's show is one of the most popular on daytime TV. It's broadcast in front of a live audience and viewed nationally. I had informed several people of the appearance, most of whom had never before seen me on television. But this time they would all be watching: my parents, uncles, aunts, cousins, and friends.

I had a lot riding on this performance because having a fortune-teller in the family is an embarrassment. It's too eccentric a profession. This was my big chance to prove I knew what I was doing; that I was genuinely learned about occult studies; that I was serious about my craft.

In between agonizing over hair and makeup, matters were further complicated when I was prompted about the most significant question I would be asked to divine. Regis wanted me to predict, using Tarot cards, the winner of the upcoming presidential election, only days away. For the second time in my career, I had a request to answer a mundane question using Tarot cards, which are normally consulted to answer personal questions. For a while I had been feeling in every fiber of my being that Bush would be the next president. But I was eager to see this premonition supported in the cards.

Around 9:30 A.M. I was brought onto the set. After briefly speaking about the history of Tarot cards and commenting on the much maligned and misunderstood Death card, I was asked by Regis to make the powerful prognosis.

"Who will win the presidential election?" he queried.

I asked Regis to pull three cards to represent Bush and three cards to represent Gore. I lined them up as he handed them to me one-by-one (See Diagram 6.1). In the Bush line-up the cards were the 4 of Pentacles, the 10 of Wands, and the Knight of Wands. For Gore the cards were The High Priestess, The Star, and the 9 of Swords. I was puzzled. From the cards' assortment, the winner was impossible to determine. There was no *clear* answer as to whom it would be. (Ironically, that *was* the correct answer, but, it didn't make any sense!)

Admittedly television is hardly a suitable forum for a serious divination. There are so many different energies pouring in and swirling around. But I also knew from years and years of observation that the messages are always coming through, and even though the cards were not giving me an obvious direct answer, nothing should ever be discredited. Nevertheless, I had no time to ponder! This was live television. Every second counts.

Although not at all conclusive, the cards for Bush did look more favorable (but not *winning*). However, my strong psychic feeling all along had been telling me Bush would be the next to inhabit the White House. So on live television, in front of all America, my family and friends, I affirmed that George W. Bush

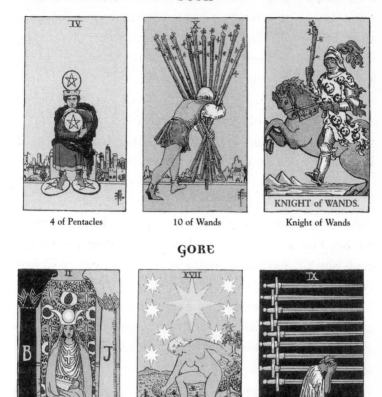

BUSH

4 of Pentacles	10 of Wands	Knight of Wands

GORE

High Priestess	The Star	9 of Swords

DIAGRAM 6.1

The 2000 Presidential Election as Portended in Tarot Cards

III would be the next president of the United State of America.

There was applause from the audience, along with some boos! Regis protected me.

"It's Halloween, you know, lighten up!" he shouted.

Pleased with my performance, my family was equally impressed. Now they were proud to have a television celebrity in the family. They rolled out the red carpet for me.

But then the unimaginable happened. The winner could not be decided! There was a confusion about the votes. For three weeks my career dangled by a dimpled chad. There isn't even a Tarot card to represent a dimpled chad!

Finally it was announced. I let out a big sigh of relief and basked in the glory of having made an outstanding and accurate prediction on *Live With Regis*. Bush was declared the winner of the presidential election. But had he *really* won?

Four months passed. I kept having a gnawing feeling that in light of what had happened, I should take another look at the tape. Maybe there was something in the cards that would explain the *confusion* surrounding the election. I had completely forgotten which cards had come up. Was I ever in for a shock! It was the cards in Gore's pile that disturbed me. The High Priestess could be interpreted as a secret, The Star as a winner, and the 9 of Swords as loss because of deception. Were the cards saying that Gore was the real winner, and it was *a secret that would never come out?*

I remembered on the show thinking that Bush's cards were more fortunate. But they did not show an easy win, and at that moment I had no idea what that meant. But here I saw it on the tape. I think the cards were portending an ominous and incredulous message. *Messages are always coming through.* I think the cards were trying to tell me something that totally transcended our framework of thinking, something too farfetched to be imaginable. After all, who would have ever thought a presidential election in the United States of America would not produce a winner?

While Bush ultimately did become the next president, there was something that happened *in between*. That is what the cards were portending; that there was going to be something very *fishy* about that election. And George W. Bush was *not* going to win fair and square. *So saith the Tarot cards!* The presidential election of 2000 will remain, without a doubt, one of our history's greatest mysteries.

I could go on and on and on. I have seen such a wide range of matters in Tarot cards: domestic violence, speeding tickets, awaiting phone messages, surprise engagements, sudden relocations, and race-horse winners. Tarot cards always *talk*. At times you will see things you cannot even believe you are seeing. The power of the cards should never be underestimated. Their revelations will always be great, profound, inspiring and awesome. It is simply up to the reader to *listen*.

Note: It is very rare to see death in the cards. NEVER predict it. If you think you see it, proceed with great caution. Suggest to the querent that now is the time to make peace with anyone she has to and to let the people she loves know how much they have meant to her and that she is glad they have been in her life.

VII

fINALE: THE LAST PICTURE SHOW

POSSIBLE MEANINGS TO THE CARDS

"My head is spinning with ideas. Now I see things in the cards I had never before seen!" Katy eagerly exclaimed.

Katy was a social worker who moonlighted as a painter and photographer. She was drawn to Tarot cards because of their rich and colorful imagery.

"I've made up so many of my own meanings, I'll have to write them down to remember."

In this final chapter there are *possible* meanings to the cards, *possible* meanings in combinations and/or positions; and, under *Notes and/or Observations*, there is a space to write your own meanings and interpretations.

DO NOT REFER TO THIS CHAPTER UNTIL THE EXERCISES IN THE FIRST 2 HOURS HAVE BEEN CORRECTLY COMPLETED!

One of the most fascinating aspects of Tarot cards is that *everyone sees something different in them*. While Marie may see one thing, Sean sees something else, or Janet and Erica may see something totally different. All are correct. But it is important to *look at the cards*. The more you look, the more you see.

This book teaches you how to develop your *own* meanings to the cards easily, spontaneously, and intuitively. Therefore these meanings are possibilities only. They are not written in stone, and this chapter is included only to help prime the pump. It is important to continue developing your own meanings and not to depend on these *possibilities*.

I have developed the majority of these meanings over the years, and *my* interpretations are of a very practical nature. However I do add a small blend of traditional meanings. Plus, there are *possible* meanings for some of the cards as they fall in proximity to each other or surround each other in a spread, as well as possible meanings for some of the cards as they may fall in various positions of certain spreads.

THE MAJOR ARCANA

THE MAGICIAN

Possible Meanings: corporate or political leadership, decision maker, executive ability, power, willpower, control, skill, mastery, self-confidence

Possible Meanings in Combinations and/or Positions: Near the 5 of Wands it may mean corporate politics; near the 7 of Wands it may mean political power struggles; in the 1st House of the Horoscope Spread, it may mean a strong, powerful, or controlling individual.

NOTES AND/OR OBSERVATIONS

THE HIGH PRIESTESS.

THE HIGH PRIESTESS

Possible Meanings: secrets, confidential information, wisdom, hidden or esoteric knowledge, intuitive or psychic ability, a reserved or private woman, behind-the-scenes influences

Possible Meanings in Combinations and/or Positions: Near The Lovers it may mean a secret romance; near The Devil it may mean a jealous enemy; near the 7 of Swords it may mean behind-the-scenes deception; in the 2nd House of the Horoscope Spread it may mean hidden money; in the 12th House of the Horoscope Spread it may mean hidden forces or espionage

NOTES AND/OR OBSERVATIONS

THE EMPRESS.

THE EMPRESS

Possible Meanings: a mother, mother-type figure (grandmother or aunt), a mother-to-be (a pregnant woman), artistic or creative ability.

Possible Meanings in Combinations and/or Positions: Near The Sun it may mean a pregnancy; near the 3 of Cups and/or the 9 of Cups it may mean a baby shower; in the *home* of any spread it may mean a mother comes for a visit; in the *home* of any spread and near the 9 of Pentacles it may mean redecorating.

NOTES AND/OR OBSERVATIONS

THE EMPEROR

Possible Meanings: a father, father-type figure (grandfather or uncle), accountant, politician, conservative statesman, lawyer, an authority figure, a strong older man

Possible Meanings in Combinations and/or Positions: Near The King of Swords it may mean a conservative accountant; near the King of Pentacles it may mean a man who adamantly or stubbornly refuses to change his beliefs; in the 9th House of the Horoscope Spread it may mean a college professor; in the *home* of any spread it may mean a father comes for a visit.

NOTES AND/OR OBSERVATIONS

THE HIEROPHANT

Possible Meanings: a priest or religious person, an accountant, a lawyer, a judge, religious matters

Possible Meanings in Combinations and/or Positions: Near The Lovers it may mean a wedding or commitment ceremony; near The Sun it may mean a baptism or bar mitzvah; in the 9th House of the Horoscope Spread it may mean religious studies; in the 9th House of the Horoscope Spread and near The World it may mean travel to a country where religion is an issue (e.g., Israel, India, Iran, Saudi Arabia).

NOTES AND/OR OBSERVATIONS

THE LOVERS

Possible Meanings: love (physical and/or spiritual), a married or engaged couple, harmony, unity

Possible Meanings in Combinations and/or Positions: Near the 2 of Cups and/or the 3 of Cups it may mean a wedding or engagement party; near The World it may mean meeting a romantic interest on a trip or a lover from afar; near The Devil it may mean jealousy in love or spousal abuse; in the 5th House of the Horoscope Spread it may mean exciting romance.

NOTES AND/OR OBSERVATIONS

THE CHARIOT.

THE CHARIOT

Possible Meanings: moving forward with a new project, success, accomplishment, focus, direction, an automobile, travel in comfort or in a luxury car

Possible Meanings in Combinations and/or Positions: Near the Knight of Swords it may mean a problem with a new car or the purchase of a new car is a necessity; near the 9 of Pentacles it may mean cosmetic work done on a car; in the 2nd House of the Horoscope Spread it may mean financial advancement.

NOTES AND/OR OBSERVATIONS

STRENGTH

Possible Meanings: strength, courage, bravery, a pet or an animal, a piece of furniture

Possible Meanings in Combinations and/or Positions: Near The Empress it may mean a strong, powerful, feminine woman; near The Magician it may mean a powerful individual in control of a situation; near the 6 of Cups it may mean children want a pet; near the 5 of Cups it may mean a pet messes up the house; near the 5 of Wands it may mean athletic strength; near the 9 of Cups it may mean strength and willpower in dieting; in the *home* of any spread and near the 3 of Cups it may mean friends come to the home for a visit with their pet.

NOTES AND/OR OBSERVATIONS

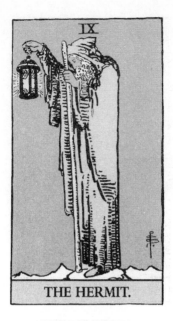

THE HERMIT.

THE HERMIT

Possible Meanings: solitude, a spiritual journey, aloneness or loneliness, reevaluating a situation, distancing oneself from a situation, research

Possible Meanings in Combinations and/or Positions: Near the 3 of Wands it may mean looking for a new job; near the 6 of Pentacles it may mean financial research; in the *home* of any spread it may mean looking for a new house or apartment.

NOTES AND/OR OBSERVATIONS

WHEEL of FORTUNE.

WHEEL OF FORTUNE

Possible Meanings: good luck or sudden good fortune, unexpected opportunity, gambling

Possible Meanings in Combinations and/or Positions: Near The Fool it may mean taking risks; near the Page of Cups it may mean a message bearing good news; near the 2 of Pentacles it may mean lucky money; in the 5th House of the Horoscope Spread it may mean luck in gambling; in the 9th House of the Horoscope Spread it may mean opportunity from faraway; in the 10th House of the Horoscope Spread it may mean a lucky career opportunity.

NOTES AND/OR OBSERVATIONS

JUSTICE.

JUSTICE

Possible Meanings: a lawyer, a judge, an accountant, legal matters, a fair decision

Possible Meanings in Combinations and/or Positions: Near the 7 of Wands it may mean legal power struggles; near The Star it may mean good news about a legal matter; in the 7th House or 9th Houses of the Horoscope Spread it may mean a lawyer or indicate legal issues; in the *home* of any spread it may mean talking to a lawyer about a legal issue relating to the home.

NOTES AND/OR OBSERVATIONS

THE HANGED MAN.

THE HANGED MAN

Possible Meanings: sacrifice, self-sacrifice, martyrdom, self-surrender, letting-go, giving something up, a co-dependent personality

Possible Meanings in Combinations and/or Positions: Near the 6 of Pentacles it may mean giving to charity or doing charity work; near Death it may mean letting go of old values; near The Lovers it may mean giving too much in a relationship; near the 8 of Pentacles and/or in the 6th House of the Horoscope Spread it may mean feeling taken advantage of in the workplace.

NOTES AND/OR OBSERVATIONS

DEATH.

DEATH

Possible Meanings: a new cycle of life, a new consciousness, changes, spiritual rebirth and/or growth, psychotherapy, clearing away psychological obstacles, unfinished business, an issue from the past comes back. (While I have clearly defined Death as ushering in a new beginning, I have, however, found it can indicate an old issue that is unfinished business or not completely concluded and resurfaces to be reworked and settled.)

Possible Meanings in Combinations and/or Positions: Near the Ace of Swords and/or the King of Swords it may mean a tax matter or talking to an accountant about a serious tax matter; near The Lovers and/or the Knight of Pentacles it may mean an old love returns; in the 8th House of the Horoscope Spread it may mean owing back taxes; in the *home* of any spread it may mean a new home or a total refurbishing.

NOTES AND/OR OBSERVATIONS

TEMPERANCE

Possible Meanings: balance, self-control, an even temper and/or calm demeanor

Possible Meanings in Combinations and/or Positions: Near The Sun it may mean a healthy, well-balanced diet; near the 2 of Pentacles it may mean a balanced budget; near Justice it may mean a fair and/or well-negotiated legal decision; near the Ace of Swords and/or the 7 of Cups it may mean medication needed for stress-related problems; in the 6th House of the Horoscope Spread it may mean a harmonious work environment.

NOTES AND/OR OBSERVATIONS

THE DEVIL.

THE DEVIL

Possible Meanings: anger, guilt, jealousy, greed, violence, revenge, vindictiveness, negative thinking and/or motivations

Possible Meanings in Combinations and/or Positions: Near the 8 of Cups it may mean walking away from evil temptations; near The Moon it may mean negative emotions; near the King of Pentacles it may mean a financially deceptive and/or dishonest man; in the 3rd House of the Horoscope Spread it may mean dangerous and/or evil neighbors or an unsavory element infiltrating the neighborhood; in the 11th House of the Horoscope Spread it may mean jealous friends.

NOTES AND/OR OBSERVATIONS

THE TOWER.

THE TOWER

Possible Meanings: a sudden change in schedule, an unexpected change in plans, a hectic schedule, unforeseeable catastrophe

Possible Meanings in Combinations and/or Positions: Near the 5 of Pentacles it may mean an unexpected and costly financial responsibility; near the 5 of Swords it may mean a sudden and violent argument; near the Wheel of Fortune it may mean sudden luck that throws one's life into chaos (*Be careful what you wish for, you just might get it!*); in the 5th House of the Horoscope Spread it may mean a whirlwind romance; in the 9th House of the Horoscope Spread it may mean an unexpected trip.

NOTES AND/OR OBSERVATIONS

THE STAR

Possible Meanings: fame, recognition, success, a promotion, inspiration

Possible Meanings in Combinations and/or Positions: Near the King of Swords it may mean good news from a doctor or an accountant; near the 9 of Pentacles it may mean a famous actress; in the 5th House of the Horoscope Spread it may mean artistic or creative inspiration; in the 10th House of the Horoscope Spread it may mean recognition in career.

NOTES AND/OR OBSERVATIONS

THE MOON.

THE MOON

Possible Meanings: intuition, psychic powers, dreams, the fourth dimension, astral projection, digestive problems, setbacks, and delays

Possible Meanings in Combinations and/or Positions: Near the King of Swords it may mean a dental problem necessitating a visit to the dentist; near the Ace of Swords it may mean a troubling message or e-mail; near the 7 of Cups it may mean alcohol and/or drug abuse; near the Knight of Swords and/or the 5 of Cups it may mean a car has an oil leak; near the 4 of Wands and/or the 3 of Pentacles and/or in the *home* of any spread it may mean plumbing repairs are needed or serious water or swimming pool problems.

NOTES AND/OR OBSERVATIONS

THE SUN.

THE SUN

Possible Meanings: joy, confidence, optimism, happiness, good health, a youthful attitude, good news, a baby

Possible Meanings in Combinations and/or Positions: Near the King of Swords it may mean good news from a doctor or a dentist; near the Ace of Cups it may mean good news in one day or one week; near the Queen of Cups it may mean a seaside resort; in the 6th House of the Horoscope Spread it may mean going on a health kick; near The World and/or in the 9th House of the Horoscope Spread it may mean travel to a warm, sunny and/or dry climate; near the 5 of Pentacles and/or in the *home* of any spread it may mean a costly heating repair; in the *home* of any spread it may mean joy in the abode.

NOTES AND/OR OBSERVATIONS

JUDGEMENT

Possible Meanings: an awakening, a revelation, a sudden awareness, renewed vitality, big news

Possible Meanings in Combinations and/or Positions: Near the High Priestess it may mean a secret comes out; near the Page of Cups it may mean someone delivers an important message; in the 3rd House of the Horoscope Spread it may mean an important message; in the 9th House of the Horoscope Spread it may mean a spiritual awakening.

NOTES AND/OR OBSERVATIONS

THE WORLD.

THE WORLD

Possible Meanings: travel, a foreign country, a faraway place, worldly success, international business

Possible Meanings in Combinations and/or Positions: Near the Knight of Pentacles it may mean a foreigner; near the 3 of Wands it may mean business expansion or business at a distance; near the 8 of Wands and/or in the 3rd House of the Horoscope Spread it may mean a message from afar; in the 9th House of the Horoscope Spread it may mean travel to a foreign country; in the *home* of any spread it may mean a home abroad or at a distance.

NOTES AND/OR OBSERVATIONS

THE FOOL.

THE FOOL

Possible Meanings: innocence, risk taking, new adventures, foolishness

Possible Meanings in Combinations and/or Positions: Near the 7 of Pentacles it may mean a speculative financial investment; near the 10 of Pentacles it may mean a risky business undertaking; near the Knight of Swords it may mean reckless driving; near the Page of Swords it may mean foolish impulsiveness; in the 5th House of the Horoscope Spread it may mean daredevil adventures.

NOTES AND/OR OBSERVATIONS

THE MINOR ARCANA

ACE of PENTACLES.

ACE OF PENTACLES

Possible Meanings: prosperity, wealth, business deals, real estate or property investment, good news about money, long-term financial planning, a business project is successful in one year

Possible Meanings in Combinations and/or Positions: Near the 6 of Pentacles it may mean sound financial advice; near the Ace of Wands and/or the 8 of Wands it may mean signing papers for business matters or real estate deals; in the 8th House of the Horoscope Spread it may mean an inheritance; near the 10 of Pentacles and/or the 4 of Wands and/or in the *home* of any spread it may mean buying or selling a home.

NOTES AND/OR OBSERVATIONS

2 OF PENTACLES

Possible Meanings: financial stability or solvency, a boat or boat ride, eyeglasses

Possible Meanings in Combinations and/or Positions: Near the Knight of Wands it may mean a motorcycle or bicycle; near the Ace of Swords it may mean an eye exam; near The Sun it may mean sunglasses; near The Chariot or the Knight of Swords it may mean a car needs a new tire or a wheel alignment; in the 3rd House of the Horoscope Spread it may mean money is sent in the mail.

NOTES AND/OR OBSERVATIONS

3 OF PENTACLES

Possible Meanings: an artist, an artisan, a church, repairs or work being done in the home, a class, a study group

Possible Meanings in Combinations and/or Positions: Near the 3 of Cups it may mean a theater group or performing in a play; near the 5 of Wands it may mean a dance or an exercise class; near The Chariot it may mean repair work on a car; in the 6th House of the Horoscope Spread it may mean a refurbishing of the workplace; in the 9th House of the Horoscope Spread it may mean study abroad.

NOTES AND/OR OBSERVATIONS

4 OF PENTACLES

Possible Meanings: saving money, economizing, frugality, hard work for low wages

Possible Meanings in Combinations and/or Positions: Near the 6 of Swords it may mean low-budget travel; near the 8 of Pentacles it may mean building financially for one's own business; near The Hanged Man it may mean making financial sacrifices; in the 1st House of the Horoscope Spread it may mean a frugal or selfish individual.

NOTES AND/OR OBSERVATIONS

5 Of PENTACLES

Possible Meanings: financial loss, financial worry, bad investments

Possible Meanings in Combinations and/or Positions: Near the Ace of Swords it may mean overextension of credit or excessive use of credit cards; near the 10 of Cups and/or the 10 of Pentacles and/or in the *home* of any spread it may mean a door or window is broken; near The Moon and/or the 5 of Cups and/or in the *home* of any spread it may mean a plumbing or water problem in the bathroom or kitchen, a leak must be repaired, or a problem with a swimming pool.

NOTES AND/OR OBSERVATIONS

6 of pentacles

Possible Meanings: making charitable donations, giving or asking for financial advice, borrowing or lending money

Possible Meanings in Combinations and/or Positions: Near the King of Swords, King of Pentacles, or Justice it may mean financial advice from an accountant or lawyer; near the 5 of Swords and/or the 7 of Cups it may mean dishonest or deceptive financial advice; in the 11th House of the Horoscope Spread it may mean financial advice from a friend.

NOTES AND/OR OBSERVATIONS

7 Of PENTACLES

Possible Meanings: long-term investments, dividends, or interest from investments, financial rewards, restructuring one's portfolio, satisfaction from work efforts

Possible Meanings in Combinations and/or Positions: Near the 6 of Cups it may mean gardening or farming; near the 10 of Cups and/or the 10 of Pentacles and/or the Ace if Pentacles it may mean buying a farm; in the 9th House of the Horoscope Spread it may mean saving money for travel or education; in the *home* or any spread it may mean investing money for home improvement.

NOTES AND/OR OBSERVATIONS

8 of pentacles

Possible Meanings: work opportunities, employment, self-employment, hard work, a craftsman

Possible Meanings in Combinations and/or Positions: Near the 3 of Wands it may mean work opportunities from a distance; near the Ace of Swords it may mean a message in one hour, one day, or one week about employment; near the 7 of Wands it may mean power struggles at work; near the 4 of Wands and/or in the *home* of any spread it may mean a home office; in the *home* of any spread it may mean repair work in the home.

NOTES AND/OR OBSERVATIONS

9 Of PENTACLES

Possible Meanings: a new self-image, a shopping spree, expensive tastes, a lady of leisure, enjoying luxurious and material comforts.

Possible Meanings in Combinations and/or Positions: Near the Queen of Cups and/or The Empress it may mean a complete makeover or new hairstyle; near the 3 of Cups it may mean buying a new dress for a party; near the 8 of Wands it may mean mail order clothing; in the *home* or any spread it may mean redecorating the home.

NOTES AND/OR OBSERVATIONS

IO Of pENTACLES

Possible Meanings: a shop, a boutique, a restaurant, a department store, corporate headquarters, an office, an expensive house

Possible Meanings in Combinations and/or Positions: Near the 3 of Swords it may mean business worries; near the 9 of Cups it may mean dinner at a four-star restaurant; near the 3 of Cups it may mean a party in a restaurant or catering hall; in the 2nd House of the Horoscope Spread it may mean investing money in a business.

NOTES AND/OR OBSERVATIONS

PAGE of PENTACLES.

PAGE OF PENTACLES

Possible Meanings: a student, research, analyzing research, study, a friend from the past comes back, an old and valuable object (antique or painting), history, computer technology, technical writing

Possible Meanings in Combinations and/or Positions: Near the 3 of Cups it may mean a reunion with old friends; near the 3 of Pentacles it may mean a college class; near The Hermit it may mean researching history; in the 12th House of the Horoscope Spread it may mean undercover investigation or classified research.

NOTES AND/OR OBSERVATIONS

KNIGHT of PENTACLES.

KNIGHT OF PENTACLES

Possible Meanings: an expensive or foreign car, publishing, art history, a computer, art or antique investment, the *old country* or *old world* style, property investment, expensive furniture

Possible Meanings in Combinations and/or Positions: Near the 5 of Wands it may mean betting on horses; near the Ace of Pentacles it may mean buying a race horse; near The Lovers or the 2 of Cups it may mean the return of an old love; in the 10th House of the Horoscope Spread it may mean doing foreign business.

NOTES AND/OR OBSERVATIONS

QUEEN of PENTACLES.

QUEEN Of PENTACLES

Possible Meanings: an introspective woman, an actress, an artistic woman, an intellectual woman, a business woman, working at a computer, reading a book

Possible Meanings in Combinations and/or Positions: Near the 8 of Wands it may mean a professional writer; in the 6th House of the Horoscope Spread it may mean secretarial work; in the 12th House of the Horoscope Spread it may mean a woman who handles confidential information.

NOTES AND/OR OBSERVATIONS

KING of PENTACLES.

KING OF PENTACLES

Possible Meanings: an older man, a wealthy man, a fatherly type, a business advisor, a stubborn man set in his ways, a controlling man

Possible Meanings in Combinations and/or Positions: Near the 5 of Wands it may mean business negotiations; near the 3 of Pentacles it may mean a business meeting; near the 2 of Swords and/or the 7 of Cups it may mean an older man under stress and/or on medication; in the 7th House of the Horoscope Spread it may mean an older husband; in the *home* of any spread it may mean a landlord.

NOTES AND/OR OBSERVATIONS

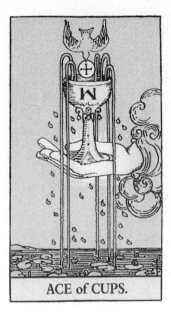

ACE OF CUPS

Possible Meanings: joy, happiness, love, emotional fulfillment, good news in one day or one week

Possible Meanings in Combinations and/or Positions: Near the Knight of Cups it may mean a message is delivered in one day or one week; near the 6 of Cups it may mean gift-giving; near the Queen of Cups it may mean receiving a gift of jewelry; in the 5th House of the Horoscope Spread it may mean creative fulfillment.

NOTES AND/OR OBSERVATIONS

2 of cups

Possible Meanings: a marriage, a wedding, a love affair, a partnership or a relationship, a commitment, harmony, a corporation

Possible Meanings in Combinations and/or Positions: Near the Ace of Pentacles it may mean a business partnership; near the 7 of Swords it may mean a cheating spouse; near the 7 of Pentacles it may mean joint financial investments; in the *home* of any spread it may mean a married couple comes for a visit.

NOTES AND/OR OBSERVATIONS

3 OF CUPS

Possible Meanings: a party, a celebration, friends, dancing

Possible Meanings in Combinations and/or Positions: Near the 9 of Cups it may mean a dinner party; near The Devil it may mean jealous friends; near the 5 of Wands it may mean manipulative friends; near the 10 of Pentacles and/or in the 10th House of the Horoscope Spread it may mean a big company or large corporation; in the *home* of any spread it may mean friends come to the home for a visit or a party.

NOTES AND/OR OBSERVATIONS

4 OF CUPS

Possible Meanings: decisions to be made, indecisiveness, daydreaming, meditation, imagination, laziness, inertia or inactivity

Possible Meanings in Combinations and/or Positions: Near the 7 of Cups and/or 7 of Swords it may mean drug and/or alcohol abuse; near The Lovers it may mean a fantasy lover; in the 5th House of the Horoscope Spread it may mean a creative idea or artistic inspiration; in the 6th House of the Horoscope Spread it may mean contemplating a new job.

NOTES AND/OR OBSERVATIONS

5 OF CUPS

Possible Meanings: disappointment, sadness, loss and suffering, depression

Possible Meanings in Combinations and/or Positions: Near the Queen of Cups it may mean the loss of a piece of jewelry; near the 6 of Cups it may mean the loss of a friend; near The Sun it may mean all is *not* lost; near the 10 of Pentacles it may mean corporate bankruptcy; in the 2nd House of the Horoscope Spread it may mean financial loss.

NOTES AND/OR OBSERVATIONS

6 of cups

Possible Meanings: siblings, relatives, children playing, friends, friendships, gifts, gardening, sharing

Possible Meanings in Combinations and/or Positions: Near the 3 of Cups it may mean a children's party; near the 5 of Wands it may mean children's games; near the Ace of Pentacles it may mean friendships have endured since childhood; near the 4 of Cups it may mean reevaluating a friendship; in the 3rd House of the Horoscope Spread and/or near the 5 of Swords it may mean sibling rivalry.

NOTES AND/OR OBSERVATIONS

7 of cups

Possible Meanings: confusion, delusion, deception, identity crisis, lack of confidence, feelings of inadequacy, overactive imagination, drug and/or alcohol abuse

Possible Meanings in Combinations and/or Positions: Near the 5 of Pentacles it may mean financial deception; near The Moon it may mean hallucinations; near the 2 of Cups it may mean confusion about a relationship; near the 2 of Swords it may mean a reaction to medication; in the 1st House of the Horoscope Spread it may mean a confused self-image; in the 3rd House of the Horoscope Spread it may mean confusing rumors and gossip going around.

NOTES AND/OR OBSERVATIONS

8 of cups

Possible Meanings: turning away from superficiality, looking for meaning in life, uncompromising of one's values, dieting, a recovering alcoholic

Possible Meanings in Combinations and/or Positions: Near the Hanged Man it may mean refusing to be taken advantage of; near the 5 of Swords it may mean walking away from an argument; in the 7th House of the Horoscope Spread it may mean leaving an emotionally empty or unfulfilling relationship.

NOTES AND/OR OBSERVATIONS

9 of cups

Possible Meanings: wish fulfillment, a wish is granted, good luck, satisfaction, eating well, cooking

Possible Meanings in Combinations and/or Positions: Near the 7 of Cups and/or The Moon it may mean a junk food binge; near the Ace of Swords it may mean following a restricted diet; near the 3 of Swords and/or The Moon it may mean digestive upsets; near The Tower it may mean unexpected good luck; in the 7th House of the Horoscope Spread it may mean fulfillment in a relationship; in the 10th House of the Horoscope Spread it may mean luck in career.

NOTES AND/OR OBSERVATIONS

10 OF CUPS

Possible Meanings: a new home, a modest home, redecorating, a happy family life

Possible Meanings in Combinations and/or Positions: Near the Queen of Cups and/or The Moon it may mean a home by water; near The Hermit it may mean looking for a new dwelling; near the Ace of Wands and/or the 8 of Wands it may mean signing papers for a new home or signing a new lease; in the 6th House or the 10th House of the Horoscope Spread it may mean a new office or a new location for a business.

NOTES AND/OR OBSERVATIONS

PAGE of CUPS.

PAGE OF CUPS

Possible Meanings: a student, a poet, a musician, an emotional individual

Possible Meanings in Combinations and/or Positions: Near The Lovers it may mean an infatuation; near the 8 of Pentacles it may mean an internship; near The Star it may mean recognition of an original and creative enterprise; near the 6 of Cups it may mean a baby-sitting job; near the 2 of Pentacles it may mean going fishing in a boat; near The Fool it may mean immaturity; in the 6th House or the 10th House of the Horoscope Spread it may mean one's first job.

NOTES AND/OR OBSERVATIONS

KNIGHT of CUPS.

KNIGHT Of CUPS

Possible Meanings: a message, a letter, a phone call, a voice mail, an e-mail, an invitation, a messenger

Possible Meanings in Combinations and/or Positions: Near the Ace of Cups it may mean a message containing good news; near the 6 of Wands it may mean contracts or papers being mailed; near the 5 of Swords it may mean an angry message or phone call; in the *home* of any spread it may mean a message coming to the home.

NOTES AND/OR OBSERVATIONS

QUEEN of CUPS.

QUEEN OF CUPS

Possible Meanings: a loving wife and/or mother, a woman who likes to cook and sew, a hair stylist or makeup artist, cosmetics, jewelry

Possible Meanings in Combinations and/or Positions: Near the 9 of Pentacles it may mean women's accessories; near the 4 of Wands it may mean a vacation home on the beach; near the Ace of Swords it may mean cosmetic surgery; near the 8 of Pentacles and/or in the 5th House of the Horoscope Spread it may mean artistic work that is profitable.

NOTES AND/OR OBSERVATIONS

KING of CUPS.

KING OF CUPS

Possible Meanings: a sensitive or emotional man, a man without ambition or direction, an artistic man

Possible Meanings in Combinations and/or Positions: Near The Devil it may mean a man who suppresses anger; near the 9 of Wands it may mean a suspicious man; near the 8 of Swords it may mean a man who is uncertain about his life direction; in the 5th House of the Horoscope Spread it may mean a highly creative but unfocused man.

NOTES AND/OR OBSERVATIONS

ACE of WANDS.

ACE Of WANDS

Possible Meanings: a new project, a creative enterprise, a new beginning, a message about work or business, papers to be signed

Possible Meanings in Combinations and/or Positions: Near The High Priestess it may mean classified papers; near the 2 of Pentacles it may mean money comes in the mail; near the 10 of Pentacles it may mean the development of a new department in a corporation; near the 3 of Pentacles it may mean the development of a new product; in the 6th House or 10th House of the Horoscope Spread it may mean a new business or work venture.

NOTES AND/OR OBSERVATIONS

2 Of WANDS

Possible Meanings: research of any kind, researching new opportunities for business growth or new territory for development, looking into opportunities at a distance (usually a westerly direction)

Possible Meanings in Combinations and/or Positions: Near The Sun it may mean contemplating travel to a warm sunny climate (e.g., California or Florida); near the Ace of Swords it may mean doing research on the Internet; near The Hermit it may mean an intense search or research; in the 2nd House of the Horoscope Spread it may mean researching financial opportunities; in the 5th House of the Horoscope Spread it may mean researching vacation spots.

NOTES AND/OR OBSERVATIONS

3 Of WANDS

Possible Meanings: reviewing business matters, planning business expansion, industry

Possible Meanings in Combinations and/or Positions: Near the 7 of Cups it may mean uncertainty about business growth; near the 4 of Wands it may mean setting up an office in another city; near The Tower it may mean unexpected business developments; in the *home* of any spread it may mean moving a distance for a new job.

NOTES AND/OR OBSERVATIONS

4 Of WANDS

Possible Meanings: a home, an apartment, a vacation home, a garage, an additional wing to a house

Possible Meanings in Combinations and/or Positions: Near the 2 of Wands it may mean looking for a new apartment or a vacation home; near the Ace of Pentacles it may mean real estate as an investment; near The Hanged Man it may mean a vacation home is a burden; in the *home* of any spread it may mean a new home or redecorating.

NOTES AND/OR OBSERVATIONS

5 Of WANDS

Possible Meanings: business negotiations, competition, a sporting event, team sports, working out, exercising, manipulation

Possible Meanings in Combinations and/or Positions: Near Strength it may mean a disciplined workout program; near Justice it may mean legal wrangling; near the 5 of Swords and/or 7 of Swords it may mean a con game; near the 7 of Wands it may mean political power struggles; near The Moon and/or in the 5th House of the Horoscope Spread it may mean swimming and/or water sports (e.g., scuba diving or surfing); in the 7th House of the Horoscope Spread it may mean a manipulative partner.

NOTES AND/OR OBSERVATIONS

6 OF WANDS

Possible Meanings: signing papers, business correspondence, a writer, advertising, letters, messages, faxes, e-mail

Possible Meanings in Combinations and/or Positions: Near The Hierophant it may mean religious writing; near Justice it may mean legal documents; near the Knight of Pentacles it may mean publishing books and/or newspaper or magazine articles; near the 2 of Pentacles it may mean payment for writing; near The Star it may mean a famous writer; in the 10th House of the Horoscope Spread it may mean a writing career.

NOTES AND/OR OBSERVATIONS

7 Of WANDS

Possible Meanings: power struggles, fighting, office politics, surrounded by controlling or difficult people, overwhelmed by such major priorities that details become unimportant

Possible Meanings in Combinations and/or Positions: Near the 3 of Cups and/or the 6 of Cups it may mean controlling friends; near the 5 of Swords it may mean violent power struggles; near the 2 of Pentacles it may mean a high-pressured sales pitch; in the 8th House of the Horoscope Spread it may mean a debt collector or a loan shark; in the 12th House of the Horoscope Spread it may mean behind-the-scenes manipulation by a secret enemy.

NOTES AND/OR OBSERVATIONS

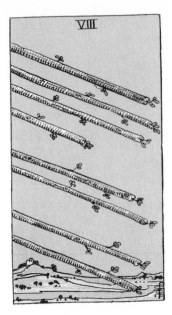

8 Of WANDS

Possible Meanings: air travel over land, travel for business, business papers and/or contracts, papers coming from a distance, business growth

Possible Meanings in Combinations and/or Positions: Near The Empress it may mean a message from a mother at a distance; near The Lovers it may mean a long-distance relationship; near the Ace of Swords it may mean insurance papers; near the 2 of Cups it may mean a prenuptial agreement; near the 6 of Wands it may mean many papers are being signed; near the Ace of Pentacles it may mean a will is signed; in the 11th House of the Horoscope Spread it may mean messages from faraway friends.

NOTES AND/OR OBSERVATIONS

9 Of WANDS

Possible Meanings: suspicion, caution, surrounded by jealousy, a clever or shrewd individual who should not be underestimated

Possible Meanings in Combinations and/or Positions: Near the 6 of Cups and The Empress it may mean an overly protective mother; near the 6 of Pentacles it may mean suspicions about money advice; near The Lovers and/or the 2 of Cups it may mean a lover or spouse is suspected of cheating; in the 11th House of the Horoscope Spread it may mean doubting one's friends are sincere.

NOTES AND/OR OBSERVATIONS

10 Of WANDS

Possible Meanings: overburdened with responsibility, worry, an independent individual

Possible Meanings in Combinations and/or Positions: Near The Tower it may mean unexpected extra responsibility; near the 8 of Pentacles it may mean doing everyone else's job; near The Empress it may mean having to care for a mother; in the 2nd House of the Horoscope Spread it may mean overburdened with financial responsibility; near The Hanged Man and/or the 5 of Pentacles and/or in the 6th House of the Horoscope Spread it may mean overworked, unappreciated, and underpaid.

NOTES AND/OR OBSERVATIONS

PAGE of WANDS.

PAGE OF WANDS

Possible Meanings: planting seeds for a new project or a new undertaking (possibly in an underdeveloped area), slow and steady growth, an innovative entrepreneur

Possible Meanings in Combinations and/or Positions: Near the 7 of Pentacles it may mean beginning a slow growing but lucrative enterprise; near The Fool it may mean taking a calculated risk; near the 3 of Pentacles it may mean starting a new course or changing one's major; in the 1st House of the Horoscope Spread it may mean an initiator or a leader.

NOTES AND/OR OBSERVATIONS

KNIGHT of WANDS.

KNIGHT Of WANDS

Possible Meanings: a new car, a fast mover, an adventurer, a driver, going west

Possible Meanings in Combinations and/or Positions: Near the Knight of Swords it may mean a problem with a new car; near the 8 of Pentacles it may mean driving to work; near The Sun it may mean driving westerly to a dry sunny climate (e.g., California, Arizona, or Colorado); near the 5 of Wands it may mean cross-country skiing; in the 3rd House of the Horoscope Spread it may mean driving in the neighborhood; in the 6th House of the Horoscope Spread it may mean one whose occupation is driving (e.g., a taxi or truck driver).

NOTES AND/OR OBSERVATIONS

QUEEN of WANDS.

QUEEN Of WANDS

Possible Meanings: a creative woman, a psychic woman, an honest woman, a business woman, a writer, woman's intuition, a cat lover or a cat

Possible Meanings in Combinations and/or Positions: Near Strength it may mean a big cat or pets; near the 5 of Wands it may mean an athletic woman; near The Magician it may mean a powerful woman who is a decision maker; near the King of Swords it may mean a woman doctor; near The Hierophant and/or in the 9th House of the Horoscope Spread it may mean a nun or a very religious woman.

NOTES AND/OR OBSERVATIONS

KING of WANDS.

KING Of WANDS

Possible Meanings: a creative man, an enterprising man, a self-absorbed man, a long-range planner, inattentive to details

Possible Meanings in Combinations and/or Positions: Near the 3 of Wands it may mean a man with far-reaching goals; near the 9 of Pentacles it may mean a well-dressed man; near the 9 of Cups it may mean a proud man; near Judgement it may mean a politically idealistic man; in the 8th House of the Horoscope Spread it may mean a man who creatively invests his clients' money or restructures bankrupt companies.

NOTES AND/OR OBSERVATIONS

ACE OF SWORDS

Possible Meanings: papers to be signed for insurance, taxes, or an estate; a driver's license, voice mail, a fax, an e-mail

Possible Meanings in Combinations and/or Positions: Near the Queen of Cups it may mean cosmetic surgery; near The Chariot and/or Justice it may mean a parking ticket or speeding violation; near The Sun and/or the King of Swords it may mean good news from a doctor or a dentist; near the King of Swords it may mean bad news from an accountant or problems with taxes; near the King of Swords and/or the 5 of Swords it may mean a brush with the law; in the 8th House of the Horoscope Spread it may mean credit or tax problems.

NOTES AND/OR OBSERVATIONS

2 Of SWORDS

Possible Meanings: indecision, worry, a stalemate, stress, tension, tuning in to intuition, being pulled in two directions, headaches, medication

Possible Meanings in Combinations and/or Positions: Near the Ace of Swords it may mean worry about credit or debt; near The Sun it may mean medication will improve a health condition; near the 5 of Cups it may mean a stress-related condition is relieved by medication; near the 7 of Pentacles it may mean indecision about financial matters; near the 9 of Swords and/or The Moon it may mean nightmares requiring sleep medication; in the 12th House of the Horoscope Spread it may mean obsessive worries.

NOTES AND/OR OBSERVATIONS

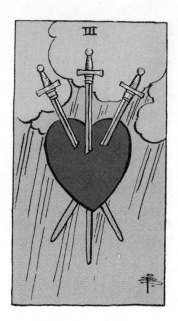

3 Of SWORDS

Possible Meanings: sorrow, sadness, disappointment, emotional suffering and loss, arguing, political strife, heartburn, and/or indigestion

Possible Meanings in Combinations and/or Positions: Near the 2 of Swords it may mean heartburn requiring medication; near The Moon it may mean severe digestive problems; near The Lovers it may mean disappointment in romance or a breakup; near the 7 of Cups it may mean disillusionment; near the 6 of Wands it may mean stress over contracts or papers to be signed; in the 12th House of the Horoscope Spread it may mean emotional alienation.

NOTES AND/OR OBSERVATIONS

4 OF SWORDS

Possible Meanings: recuperation, recovery, rest, waiting patiently, *sleeping on it* before making a decision, a funeral

Possible Meanings in Combinations and/or Positions: Near the King of Pentacles it may mean business delays; near the 4 of Cups it may mean slow meditative evaluation before making decisions; near The Sun and/or the Ace of Swords it may mean recuperating after surgery; near The Hierophant it may mean contemplating a monastic life; in the *atmosphere* of the Celtic Cross Spread it may mean feeling lonely.

NOTES AND/OR OBSERVATIONS

5 Of SWORDS

Possible Meanings: a violent argument, a crime, an abrupt change in plans

Possible Meanings in Combinations and/or Positions: Near the Knight of Swords it may mean a car accident or reckless driving; near The Devil it may mean an angry, bitter, or sarcastic person; near the 3 of Cups it may mean an argument with friends; near the 7 of Swords it may mean a violent crime and/or robbery; in the 3rd House of the Horoscope Spread it may mean violence in the neighborhood or an angry phone message.

NOTES AND/OR OBSERVATIONS

6 OF SWORDS

Possible Meanings: travel by water, travel by air (over water), travel over a bridge, travel by subway or train, travel on a highway (possibly east or northeast) or local travel, personality transformations or changes

Possible Meanings in Combinations and/or Positions: Near The World it may mean a long airplane trip; near The Chariot it may mean a long car journey; near The Empress it may mean a trip to visit a mother; near The Tower and/or the 10 of Wands and/or The Hanged Man and/or in the 3rd House of the Horoscope Spread it may mean a sudden, unexpected change in schedule requiring a short journey to fulfill a dutiful obligation or to do someone a favor.

NOTES AND/OR OBSERVATIONS

7 Of SWORDS

Possible Meanings: a thief, a spy, a malicious gossiper, making secret plans, deception, behind the scenes manipulation, losing a set of keys

Possible Meanings in Combinations and/or Positions: Near the Queen of Swords it may mean a gossipy woman; near The High Priestess it may mean the planning of highly secretive operations; near Judgement it may mean a secret comes out; in the 12th House of the Horoscope Spread it may mean a corporate takeover or a coup; in the *home* of any spread it may mean a dangerous person lurking around the home.

NOTES AND/OR OBSERVATIONS

8 OF SWORDS

Possible Meanings: restrictions, prison, incarceration, feeling trapped in a bad situation, trusting one's intuition

Possible Meanings in Combinations and/or Positions: Near the 4 of Pentacles it may mean financial restrictions; near Justice it may mean legal restrictions; near the Ace of Wands it may mean trying to find the way out of a bad situation; in the 7th House of the Horoscope Spread it may mean feeling trapped in a marriage; near The Tower and/or in the 12th House of the Horoscope Spread it may mean long-term incarceration.

NOTES AND/OR OBSERVATIONS

9 Of SWORDS

Possible Meanings: illness, worry, nightmares, insomnia, a female disorder, or female surgery

Possible Meanings in Combinations and/or Positions: Near The Moon it may mean nightmares or insomnia because of digestive disturbances; near The Empress it may mean a miscarriage or female illness; near the Ace of Cups it may mean a disturbing message; near the 4 of Swords it may mean sorrow over the loss of a loved one; in the 10th House of the Horoscope Spread it may mean worry over one's reputation.

NOTES AND/OR OBSERVATIONS

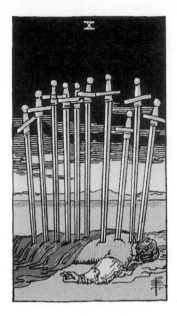

IO Of SWORDS

Possible Meanings: said to be the *worst* card in the deck, severe depression, anxiety, loss and misfortune

Possible Meanings in Combinations and/or Positions: near the 3 of Swords and/or the 7 of Cups it may mean severe emotional trauma; near Death it may mean thoughts of suicide; near the 5 of Pentacles it may financial ruin; near the 10 of Cups and The Tower it may mean loss of one's home by fire; in the 10th House of the Horoscope Spread it may mean loss of one's reputation; in the *home* of any spread it may mean mean loss of one's home.

NOTES AND/OR OBSERVATIONS

PAGE of SWORDS.

PAGE OF SWORDS

Possible Meanings: an angry young person, an impulsive young person, a headstrong youth, an immature person, a defensive individual, a fighter, a poor planner

Possible Meanings in Combinations and/or Positions: Near the 6 of Cups it may mean immature friends; near the 5 of Swords it may mean one who looks for a fight; near The Emperor it may mean anger towards the father; near the 5 of Wands it may mean a childish or senseless argument; in the 3rd House of the Horoscope Spread it may mean an immature sibling.

NOTES AND/OR OBSERVATIONS

KNIGHT of SWORDS.

KNIGHT Of SWORDS

Possible Meanings: an aggressive individual, a hostile individual, a military career

Possible Meanings in Combinations and/or Positions: Near the King of Swords it may mean an argument with a cop; near the 7 of Swords it may mean a car thief; near The Magician it may mean a ruthless or despotic personality; near The Devil it may mean a sociopath; near the 5 of Wands it may mean the martial arts; in the 2nd House of the Horoscope Spread it may mean impulsive spending.

NOTES AND/OR OBSERVATIONS

QUEEN of SWORDS.

QUEEN OF SWORDS

Possible Meanings: a cruel woman, an abrasive woman, a cutthroat woman, a woman who cannot be trusted, a woman physician, a woman stockbroker, a police woman

Possible Meanings in Combinations and/or Positions: Near The Devil it may mean a jealous and vindictive woman; near The Sun it may mean a difficulty in getting pregnant; near the 7 of Wands it may mean a controlling woman; near The High Priestess it may mean a highly secretive woman; in the 10th House of the Horoscope Spread it may mean an abusive mother.

NOTES AND/OR OBSERVATIONS

KING of SWORDS.

KING OF SWORDS

Possible Meanings: an accountant, a physician, a dentist, a lawyer, a law enforcement officer, a soldier, an insensitive man

Possible Meanings in Combinations and/or Positions: Near The Emperor it may mean a strict father; near Strength it may mean a veterinarian; near the 6 of Pentacles it may mean an aggressive financial advisor; in the 7th House of the Horoscope Spread it may mean a cold and indifferent spouse; in the 9th House of the Horoscope Spread it may mean a medical student.

NOTES AND/OR OBSERVATIONS

Celtic Cross Spread Worksheet

Date:_____

Significator: _____

1. _____
   What Covers You

2. _____
   What Crosses You

3. _____
   Above You

4. _____
   Below You

5. _____
   Behind You

6. _____
   Before You

7. _____
   You/the Querent

8. _____
   Home, Family, Friends, and/or Environment

9. _____
   Hopes and/or Fears

10. _____
    Outcome or Culmination

Notes and/or Observations: (corresponding events, feelings, etc.)

Seven Triplets or Seven Sisters Spread Worksheet

Date:_____

1._____ 2._____ 3._____
Pile 1

1._____ 2._____ 3._____
Pile 2

1._____ 2._____ 3._____
Pile 3

1._____ 2._____ 3._____
Pile 4

1._____ 2._____ 3._____
Pile 5

1._____ 2._____ 3._____
Pile 6

1._____ 2._____ 3._____
Pile 7

Notes and/or Observations: (corresponding events, feelings, etc.)

Advanced Celtic Cross Spread Worksheet

Date:_____

Significator: _____

_____

1. What Covers You

_____

2. What Crosses You

_____

3. Above You

_____

4. Below You

_____

5. Behind You

1._____ 2._____ 3._____
6. Before You

1._____ 2._____ 3._____
7. You/The Querent

1._____ 2._____ 3._____
8. Home, Family, Friends, and/or Environment

_____

9. Hopes and/or Fears

1._____ 2._____ 3._____
10. Outcome or Culmination

Notes and/or Observations: (corresponding events, feelings, etc.)

Horoscope Spread Worksheet

Date:_____

1. _____

   1st House/Querent

2. _____

   2nd House/Finances

3. _____

   3rd House/Communications

4. _____

   4th House/Home

5. _____

   5th House/Romance

6. _____

   6th House/Work, Health

7. _____

   7th House/Partners, Marriage

8. _____

   8th House/Credit

9. _____

   9th House/Education

10. _____

    10th House/Career

11. _____

    11th House/Friends

12. _____

    12th House/Secret Enemies, Danger

13. _____

    Center/General Interpretation

Notes and/or Observations: (corresponding events, feelings, etc.)

Advanced Horoscope Spread Worksheet

Date:_____

1._____   2._____   3._____
1st House

1._____   2._____   3._____
2nd House

1._____   2._____   3._____
3rd House

1._____   2._____   3._____
4th House

1._____   2._____   3._____
5th House

1._____   2._____   3._____
6th House

1._____   2._____   3._____
7th House

1._____   2._____   3._____
8th House

1._____   2._____   3._____
9th House

1._____   2._____   3._____
10th House

1._____   2._____   3._____
11th House

1._____   2._____   3._____
12th House

1._____   2._____   3._____
Center

Notes and/or Observations: (corresponding events, feelings, etc.)

Five-By-Five / Month-By-Month Spread Worksheet

Date:_____

1._____ 2._____ 3._____ 4._____ 5._____
Row 1—Past or Immediate Past

1._____ 2._____ 3._____ 4._____ 5._____
Row 2—Present, Current Month

1._____ 2._____ 3._____ 4._____ 5._____
Row 3—The Next Month

1._____ 2._____ 3._____ 4._____ 5._____
Row 4—The Following Month

1._____ 2._____ 3._____ 4._____ 5._____
Row 5—3 to 5 Months After

Notes and/or Observations: (corresponding events, feelings, etc.)

One-Year Spread Worksheet

Date:_____

Significator: _____

1. _____
   1st Month (or Current Calendar Month)

2. _____
   2nd Month

3. _____
   3rd Month

4. _____
   4th Month

5. _____
   5th Month

6. _____
   6th Month

7. _____
   7th Month

8. _____
   8th Month

9. _____
   9th Month

10. _____
    10th Month

11. _____
    11th Month

12. _____
    12th Month

Notes and/or Observations: (corresponding events, feelings, etc.)

The Horseshoe Spread Worksheet

Date:_____

1. _____
   The Past

2. _____
   The Present

3. _____
   The Immediate Future

4. _____
   The Querent and/or What the Question Is About

5. _____
   The Attitude of Another Person

6. _____
   An Obstacle

7. _____
   The Outcome

Notes and/or Observations: (corresponding events, feelings, etc.)

BIBLIOGRAPHY

Buess, Lynn M. *The Tarot and Transformation*. Lakemont, Georgia: Tarnhelm Press, 1973.

Campbell, Florence. *Your Days Are Numbered*. Ferndale, PA: The Gateway, 1931.

Cavendish, Richard. *The Black Arts*. New York: G. P. Putnam's Sons, 1967.

Douglas, Alfred. *The Tarot*. New York: Penguin Books, 1973.

Fortune, Dion. *Practical Occultism in Daily Life*. London: The Aquarian Press, 1935.

Fortune, Dion. *Psychic Self-Defence*. London: The Aquarian Press, 1930.

Gardner, Richard. *The Tarot Speaks*. London: Rigel Press, 1971.

Gray, Eden. *A Complete Guide to the Tarot*. New York: Crown Publishers, Inc., 1970.

Gray, Eden. *Mastering the Tarot*. New York: Crown Publishers, Inc., 1971.

Herrigel, Eugen. *Zen in the Art Of Archery*. New York: Pantheon Books, Inc., 1953.

The I Ching or Book of Changes. Translated by Cary F. Baynes. Princeton: Princeton University Press, 1950.

Lofthus, Myrna. *A Spiritual Approach to Astrology*. Reno: CRCS Publications, 1983.

Ouspensky, P. D. *In Search of the Miraculous*. New York: Harcourt, Brace & World, Inc., 1949.

Steinbach, Marten. *Medical Palmistry*. Secaucus: University Books, Inc., 1975.

Swami Vishnudevananda. *The Complete Illustrated Book of Yoga*. New York: Bell Publishing Company, Inc., 1960.

Webster's New World Dictionary of The American Language, College Edition. Cleveland and New York: The World Publishing Company 1953.

Tarot reader, psychic, and astrologer **Wilma Carroll** has been a practicing intuitive consultant for over 35 years. She has appeared on *Live with Regis*, *Late Show with David Letterman*, and The Learning Channel, as well as Fox News and *Good Day New York*. She has published articles in *Dell Horoscope* and *Fate Magazine*, and she has been quoted in the *Daily News*, *New York Post*, *Teen People*, and *Vibe*. Her presence has graced parties thrown by Ivana Trump, Stone Phillips, Angie Everhart, Ron Howard, and Amy Tan.

Wilma Carroll invites all readers to visit her website, www.wilmacarroll.com or correspond with her at wilma.carroll@verizon.net.

PIATKUS BOOKS

If you have enjoyed reading this book, you may be interested in other titles published by Piatkus. These include:

ISBN	Title	Author	Price
0 7499 2293 1	10 Steps to Psychic Power	Cassandra Eason	£12.99
0 7499 2459 4	5-Minute Meditator, The	Eric Harrison	£7.99
0 7499 2160 9	A Woman's Spiritual Journey	Joan Borysenko	£12.99
0 7499 1581 1	At Peace In The Light	Dannion Brinkley	£10.99
0 7499 2110 2	Balancing Your Chakras	Sonia Choquette	£9.99
0 7499 2201 X	Believing It All	Marc Parent	£9.99
0 7499 1969 8	Book Of Shadows	Phyllis Curott	£10.99
0 7499 1168 9	Care Of The Soul	Thomas Moore	£10.99
0 7499 1892 6	Channelling	Lita de Alberdi	£9.99
0 7499 1773 3	Children & The Spirit World	Linda Williamson	£8.99
0 7499 1929 9	Chinese Face and Hand Reading	J. O'Brien and M. Palmer	£8.99
0 7499 1824 1	Clear Your Clutter With Feng Shui	Karen Kingston	£7.99
0 7499 2049 1	Colour Healing Manual	Pauline Wills	£12.99
0 7499 1846 2	Colour Your Life	Howard and Dorothy Sun	£10.99
0 7499 2096 3	Colours of the Soul	June McLeod	£10.99
0 7499 2079 3	Dolphin Healing	Horace Dobbs	£10.99
0 7499 2158 7	Endorphin Effect, The	William Bloom	£12.99
0 7499 2303 2	Energy Healing For Beginners	Ruth White	£9.99
0 7499 2415 2	Everyday Karma	Carmen Harra	£9.99
0 7499 1927 2	Everyday Rituals and Ceromonies	Lorna St Aubyn	£8.99
0 7499 2143 9	Finding Fulfilment	Liz Simpson	£8.99
0 7499 2295 8	Heal Yourself	Anne Jones	£10.99
0 7499 1942 6	Healers and Healing	Roy Stemman	£8.99
0 7499 2308 3	Healing Journey, The	Matthew Manning	£12.99
0 7499 1265 0	I Ching Or Book Of Changes, The	Brian Browne Walker	£7.99
0 7499 1510 2	Journey of Self Discovery	Ambika Wauters	£8.99
0 7499 2182 X	Life on the Other Side	Sylvia Browne	£12.99
0 7499 2497 7	Living Druidry	Emma Restall Orr	£10.99
0 7499 2071 8	Living Magically	Gill Edwards	£9.99
0 7499 2339 3	Make Your Dreams Come True	Ulli Springett	£9.99
0 7499 1378 9	Many Lives, Many Masters	Brian Weiss	£9.99
0 7499 1958 2	Meditation Plan, The	Richard Lawrence	£10.50
0 7499 1979 5	One Last Time	John Edward	£9.99
0 7499 2394 6	One-Liners	Ram Dass	£4.99
0 7499 1620 6	Only Love Is Real	Brian Weiss	£9.99
0 7499 2091 2	Other Side and Back, The	Sylvia Browne	£12.99
0 7499 2089 0	Palmistry in the 21st Century	Lori Reid	£8.99
0 7499 2228 1	Past Lives, Future Healing	Sylvia Browne	£12.99
0 7499 1377 0	Past Lives, Present Dreams	Denise Linn	£8.99
0 7499 2392 X	Peace Angels	Antoinette Sampson	£6.99
0 7499 2064 5	Pendulum Dowsing	Cassandra Eason	£7.99
0 7499 1948 5	Power of Inner Peace, The	Diana Cooper	£10.50
0 7499 2422 5	Power of Karma, The	Mary T. Browne	£7.99

0 7499 2606 6	Psychic World of Derek Acorah, The	Derek Acorah	£7.99
0 7499 2120 X	Radionics Handbook, The	Keith Mason	£10.99
0 7499 1995 7	Reaching To Heaven	James Van Praagh	£9.99
0 7499 2338 5	Reading the Future	Sasha Fenton	£10.99
0 7499 2530 2	Reincarnation	Roy Stemman	£7.99
0 7499 1404 1	Saved By The Light	Dannion Brinkley	£9.99
0 7499 2375 X	Seven Steps to Heaven	Joyce Keller	£9.99
0 7499 2072 6	Stepping Into The Magic	Gill Edwards	£9.99
0 7499 2321 0	Sylvia Browne's Book Of Dreams	Sylvia Browne	£10.99
0 7499 2246 X	Symbol Therapy	Ulli Springett	£8.99
0 7499 1009 7	Tarot Made Easy	Nancy Garen	£12.99

All Piatkus titles are available from:

Piatkus Books Ltd, c/o Bookpost, PO Box 29, Douglas, Isle of Man, IM99 1BQ

Telephone (+44) 01624 677 237
Fax (+44) 01624 670 923
Email: bookshop@enterprise.net
Free Postage and Packing in the United Kingdom
Credit Cards accepted. All Cheques payable to Bookpost

Prices and availability are subject to change without prior notice. Allow 14 days for delivery. When placing orders, please state if you do not wish to receive any additional information.